THE MORAL
IMPERATIVE

THE MORAL IMPERATIVE

An Introduction to Ethical Judgment

SECOND EDITION

Vincent Ryan Ruggiero

State University of New York, Delhi

 MAYFIELD PUBLISHING COMPANY

Copyright © 1982, 1984 by Mayfield Publishing Company.
Copyright © 1973 by Alfred Publishing Company, Inc.
Second edition, 1984

Library of Congress Catalog Card Number: 83-061532
International Standard Book Number: 0-87484-590-4

Manufactured in the United States of America
Mayfield Publishing Company
285 Hamilton Avenue
Palo Alto, California 94301

Sponsoring editor: Franklin C. Graham
Manuscript editor: Marie Enders
Managing editor: Pat Herbst
Art director: Nancy Sears
Production manager: Cathy Willkie
Cover designer: Gary Head
Compositor: Columbia Phototype
Printer and binder: Bookcrafters

To

Vincent V. Ruggiero, my father,
Filomena Ruggiero, my grandmother,
Francis and Michael Ruggiero, my uncles, and
Edith and Bernhard Theisselmann, my "extra parents,"
whose quiet lessons and example first introduced
me to the subject of this book.

CONTENTS

I / THE CONTEXT

CHAPTER 1
The Need for Ethics

Why do we need ethics? We have laws to protect people's rights. We have religious beliefs to guide their actions. If the laws are enforced and the beliefs followed, what need have we of further rules?

CHAPTER 2
Comparing Cultures

How do we account for the fact that an action that is praised in one culture may be condemned in another? Doesn't this suggest that all moral values are relative to the culture they are found in?

CHAPTER 3
Judging Issues

Doesn't the fact of such great differences in basic ethical judgments (if not in underlying values) among cultures caution us against claiming that any culture is better than others? Isn't it a mark of ignorance to pass judgment on the morality of those who disagree with us?

CHAPTER 10

How do we deal with cases in which the consequences are not neatly separable into good and bad,
but are mixed?

CHAPTER 11

How do we determine whether a person is responsible for her or his immoral actions? Are there degrees of responsibility?

CHAPTER 12

What are the most common errors in moral reasoning? How can these errors best be avoided?

III / THE TRADITION

CHAPTER 13

When did the study of ethics begin? Who were the
great thinkers in the history of ethics? What contributions did they make?

IV / CONTEMPORARY ETHICAL
CONTROVERSIES

TO THE INSTRUCTOR

No introductory textbook can do complete justice to the subject of ethics. The best it can do is to help students develop a basic competency in ethical analysis, acquire a measure of confidence in their judgment, and stimulate enough interest in the subject that they will want to continue learning about it, formally or informally, when the final chapter is completed and the course is over. Even that relatively modest aim is difficult to achieve. The author must strike the right balance between the theoretical and the practical, breadth and depth of treatment, and rigor and relevance, so that students are challenged but not daunted.

This book is based on several specific ideas about how that crucial balance is best achieved:

The emphasis should be on DOING ethics rather than on studying the history of ethics. This does not mean that students should not become familiar with historical developments and the contributions of great ethicists. It does mean that more attention should be given to applying ethical principles to specific cases, to conducting ethical analysis. This approach, which Alfred North Whitehead termed an emphasis on principles rather than details (and which he proposed as the standard for all education), is the same approach that many educators are recommending to promote the development of critical thinking skills in philosophy, the social sciences, and the humanities.

Careful attention should be given to overcoming students' intellectual impediments to ethical analysis. Today's students have been exposed to numerous misconceptions about ethical analysis—indeed, about thinking in general. For example, it is fashionable today to regard all value judgments as undemocratic. This fashion has led many students to the belief that whatever one *feels* is right is by that very fact right ("right for me," as the saying goes). Even when they manage to avoid that notion, many students adopt other erroneous notions—for instance, that the majority view is necessarily the best view, or that morality is a religious matter only, without any secular dimension. Unless students get beyond such crippling notions, their efforts at ethical analysis are unlikely to be effective and meaningful.

The fundamental concerns in ethical analysis should be presented first, and more complex concerns reserved, wherever possible, until later. This may seem too obvious to state. Yet it is a consideration that many textbooks in ethics (and in other subjects) ignore. Such textbooks present a concept in detail, with all the conflicting interpretations of it that have been advanced by various ethical schools. This conflicting information can paralyze student effort. Instead of applying the concept in their work, as the authors intend, students often think, "If the experts disagree, how can I be expected to make sense of this?" The time for identifying complexities is after students have been introduced to the basic concept and have become comfortable applying it in their analyses.

Special Features of This Book

The influence of the foregoing ideas accounts for certain features that distinguish this book from many other introductory ethics texts. The more significant of these features are the following:

Chapter Length Short chapters allow students to spend less time reading and underlining and more time analyzing ethical problems. More conscientious students gain an additional benefit from the brevity of the chapters. These students are able to read each chapter more than once and thereby master the material better than they would with a long chapter.

Organization   The history of ethics and the contributions of great ethicists are presented at the end of the book (in Chapter 13) rather than at the beginning or throughout. This arrangement reflects the author's experience that most introductory students learn ethical analysis better when they are not burdened with names and dates and details of ethical systems. Showing students how Plato, Kant, and Mill approached an ethical issue and then asking them to analyze an issue themselves is very much like showing them a professional athlete performing and then saying, "Now, let's see how you perform." Both situations are intimidating; students are put in a competitive situation (whether it is called that or not) in which they cannot compete. In ethics, as in sports, it is better to postpone introducing students to "the professionals" until they have gained a little experience and confidence.

This format does not diminish the importance of ethical history. On the contrary, students are better able to appreciate and remember historical contributions after they have grappled with problems themselves and pondered the question of how to judge them. (In cases where course syllabi require that historical material be presented first, instructors can begin with Chapter 13 and then proceed with Chapters 1, 2, and so on.)

Critical Thinking   Chapter 12 discusses common errors in moral reasoning and ways to avoid them. This material, which both reinforces earlier chapters' cautions about misconceptions and introduces specific procedural errors that occur frequently in ethical analysis, is especially valuable in ethics courses that include a critical thinking objective.

Appendix on Writing   Today's students often arrive at college without the English proficiency that instructors expect them to have. The guide to writing included in this text can save instructors time and effort. Instead of trying to teach rhetorical skills during class or in conferences with students, instructors need only direct students to the Appendix. Students, too, benefit by being able to break the common cycle of submitting poor papers, getting poor grades, becoming frustrated, losing interest, and blaming the instructor. By knowing what is expected in their analyses of issues and, more important, how to provide it, they can devote more attention to the mastery and application of ethical principles.

The correction symbols noted in the Appendix can be used to make the evaluation of papers faster and more effective. If a paper is lacking in both coherence and development, the instructor need write nothing more than COH and DEV. Students will be able to turn to the appropriate sections of the Appendix, see what errors they have committed, and note how to avoid those errors in the future.

A Note on Student Frustration

The approach used in the early chapters of this book will be frustrating to some students. They will ask, "If it's not feelings and not majority opinion that decide the morality of an action, then what is it? Why doesn't the author tell us?" This reaction is a reflection of students' prior classroom conditioning. They expect textbooks to provide neat answers that can be swallowed and then regurgitated on a test. When asked to think, to reason out for themselves the best answers to moral problems, they naturally become anxious for a time. The activity is unfamiliar.

Whenever your students ask, "What *does* decide the morality of an action?" you will know that their minds have become engaged in the subject, that they are seeing the need for a standard other than feelings, for example, and are struggling to define it. By the time the book suggests the criteria of judgment (Chapter 7), students will be ready to learn and apply those criteria. Many, in fact, will already have anticipated the criteria in their own analyses of problems. Without realizing it, they will have been *doing* ethics.

Vincent Ryan Ruggiero

Acknowledgments

I am grateful to all who had a part in the making of this book. Special thanks go to Professor Gaston Pelletier of SUNY, Delhi College, for suggesting the title; to Don Anderson of Los Angeles Pierce College, Walter Coole of Skagit Valley College, Tom Cunningham of Grand Valley State Colleges, Carol J. Falk of Concordia College, Lawrence Finsen of the University of Redlands, John A. Kimmey, Jr., of North Texas State University, Mary F. Matthews of Illinois Central College, and Albert E. Solomon of Education and Training Consultants for their helpful suggestions for revising the manuscript; and to Franklin Graham of Mayfield Publishing Company for so ably directing the preparation of this new edition.

V.R.R.

THE MORAL
IMPERATIVE

THE SAME MORAL ISSUES that men and women have grappled with throughout history have grown ever more difficult in a society whose structures and forms are changing. And the impressive advances of science and technology have created a host of new issues.

Yet precisely at this time, when we most need a firm intellectual foundation to guide our judgment, we are confused by countless challenges to old and familiar faiths and standards.

The outlines of our very humanity are blurred by conflicting theories.

This, then, is the moral imperative of our time—to break the bonds of indecision, move beyond fad and foolishness, and address the dilemmas of modern living, sensitively and sensibly, with regard for their complexity.

THE CONTEXT

The Need for Ethics

CHAPTER 1

Why do we need ethics? We have laws to protect people's rights. We have religious beliefs to guide their actions. If the laws are enforced and the beliefs followed, what need have we of further rules?

A car speeds through a red light at a crowded intersection; a squad car begins pursuit, lights flashing and siren screaming. Two men are fighting in a bar; one pulls a knife, stabs the other, and runs out; the proprietor calls the police, who seek out the assailant. A store owner arrives at her place of business one morning and finds it has been burglarized; she reports the burglary, and detectives begin searching for clues to the burglar's identity.

Such events are unfortunately common. And there is nothing strange or unusual about the behavior of the police in response to them. In each case a law has been broken, and the police are doing their job—investigating the details of the case and apprehending suspects.

If asked where the laws came from, we would have little difficulty answering. They are made by legislators, "lawmakers," at various levels

1

of government: local, state, national. But if we were asked what the legislators based those laws on, we might have more difficulty answering. Why did they prohibit speeding through red lights, stabbing others, breaking into others' places of business and taking their property? The answer we would undoubtedly be driven to, after experiencing the frustration of groping for a more definitive response, is "Because those actions are wrong!"

With such cases, that answer would usually satisfy. Not so in all cases, however. Why can't a wage earner choose not to file an income tax return or use a different tax schedule from the one provided on the government form? Why can't people grow marijuana in their backyards or smoke it in the privacy of their own homes? To say we can't perform these actions because they are wrong is not enough, for the question that leaps forth from that response is "But *why* are they wrong?" (if, indeed, they are wrong). To answer that question we must do something more than invoke the laws themselves. We must examine the moral perspective that underlies them.

If the laws themselves were a trustworthy measure of the rightness of actions, then there could not be a bad law. Every law would of necessity be just. Yet we know that some laws (or applications of laws) are unjust despite the good intentions of lawmakers. That is, they punish behavior that does not deserve punishment, or they make unreasonable demands. The Eighteenth Amendment to the U.S. Constitution made Prohibition the law of the land . . . until the Twenty-first Amendment repealed it in the name of justice. Members of the Amish religious sect, whose way of life called for less formal schooling than the law prescribed, were judged criminals for withdrawing their children from school . . . until the U.S. Supreme Court declared the application of the law to them unjust. In New York State rape victims were required to prove they had given "earnest resistance" to the rapist . . . until the state legislature removed that unreasonable provision from the law.[1]

Laws are, in large part, a reflection of a country's conclusions about right and wrong. Such conclusions are separate from the law and precede it. They are not fixed and immutable, but alive and growing, changing as imperceptibly as our culture changes, responding to

2

its challenges. They provide us all, including legislators and jurists, with a perspective from which to evaluate and classify actions, approving some and disapproving others.

Ethics Defined

Ethics is the study of right and wrong conduct. In the scientific sense, it is a descriptive discipline, involving the collection and interpretation of data on what people from various cultures believe, without any consideration for the appropriateness or reasonableness of those beliefs. In the philosophical sense, the sense that concerns us, ethics is a two-sided discipline. One side, *normative ethics,* answers specific moral questions, determining what is reasonable and therefore what people should believe. (The term *normative* means setting "norms" or guidelines.) The other side of philosophical ethics, *metaethics,* examines ethical systems to appraise their logical foundations and internal consistency.

The focus of ethics is moral situations—that is, *those situations in which there is a choice of behavior involving human values* (those qualities that are regarded as good and desirable). Thus whether we watch TV at a friend's house or at our own is not a moral issue. But whether we watch TV at a friend's house without his or her knowledge and approval is a moral issue. Similarly, filling out an application for a job is a morally neutral act. But deciding whether to tell the truth on the application is a moral decision. An ethicist observes the choices people make in various moral situations and draws conclusions about those choices. An ethical system is a set of coherent ideas that result from those conclusions and form an overall moral perspective.

Ethicists are not lawmakers. They are neither elected nor appointed. Their only authority is the force of reasonableness in their judgments. Their words, unlike those of lawmakers, do not prescribe what must or must not be done. They merely suggest what *ought* to be done. If people violate their own or their society's moral code, no ethics enforcement officer will try to apprehend them—though if their action also violates a law, a law enforcement agency may do so.

Law enforcement, of course, extends beyond apprehension of

alleged criminals. It includes the formal trial and judgment of guilt or innocence, and there are degrees of guilt. A person who carries out a carefully planned murder is charged with a more serious crime than is a person who strikes and kills another in spontaneous, blind rage. In fact, if the individual in the latter example is judged to have been insane, he or she may go entirely unpunished.

The idea of varying degrees of responsibility for one's actions is applied in ethics, too. Although there are no courts of ethics as there are courts of law, and no formal pronouncements of guilt or innocence in actual cases, the ethicist nevertheless is interested in the question, "Under what circumstances is a person to be counted culpable?" (In applied law, as in law*making*, the thoughts of ethicists provide a foundation for legal judgments.)

Ethics and Religious Belief

What is the relation between ethics and religious belief? Isn't distinguishing between right and wrong a religious matter? And shouldn't the distinction therefore be made in a religious context? The answer depends on several considerations. First, it depends on what we mean by a "religious matter." If we mean morality is a spiritual affair in the sense that it reflects the quality of one's character, then yes, the context should be religious. But if by "religious matter" we mean "subject to a particular institutional religion and its doctrine," the answer is no, for no one religion can legitimately claim sole jurisdiction over the consideration of right and wrong. That consideration is a human matter, a subject of human interest independent of any religious belief.

It is, of course, as acceptable as it is common for a religious group to believe that its moral values are better than those of others. But if any group wants to persuade others of such a belief, it must seek some common ground, some mutually shared approach to ethical issues. If it wishes to extend its dialogue to those with very different religious beliefs or no religious belief, then it must adopt its criteria of judgment very carefully.

It is not very helpful, for example, to judge actions by the criterion of whether they "please or offend God." The question that naturally arises is "How do you know whether they do or not?" And the two most common answers serve more to close off ethical inquiry than to promote it: One is "Because the Bible (or Koran, and so forth) says so." The other is "This is my belief." If we wish to pursue the matter further, we are placed in the position of having to challenge the Bible or to invade the very private domain of the other person's belief.

In addition, both answers are based on erroneous notions. Saying "the Bible says so" suggests that the Bible is a simple book that doesn't admit of more than a single interpretation. Yet biblical scholarship clearly demonstrates that it is complex and open to numerous interpretations. Saying "this is my belief" implies that no aspect of a person's belief can be shallow or mistaken, that in religious matters there is no room for growth and development. The lives of the saints and holy men and women of the world's religions disprove any such notion.

Some ethical questions cannot be adequately answered by reference to religious beliefs alone. Take, for example, the case of a person's pondering this question: "Since I no longer accept some of the major teachings of the church I was raised in, is it morally right for me to remain a member? What ought I to do?" The question is by no means an easy one, though it may appear so. Whatever approach the individual might use in answering it, the teachings of his or her religion would hardly be the definitive measure, for they are an integral part of the question. *Using them would be equivalent to affirming them.*

In other cases, religious beliefs may speak directly but too narrowly. Consider this case. A schoolteacher is found to belong to a mate-swapping club. The school board decides that the teacher's behavior, though clearly a private matter, is likely to be a source of scandal to the community. Therefore, they summarily dismiss the teacher. The question under consideration is, "Was the board's decision ethically justifiable?" To answer it fairly, we should approach it openmindedly. Yet if our religious belief includes strong prohibitions against adultery and scandal, but virtually none against job discrimination because of lifestyle, we might approach the question with our minds made up. We might be unable to consider the possibility that the teacher was wronged.

5

Most religious thinkers recognize the error of judging moral issues merely by religious belief. They realize the importance of discussing them in a way that is meaningful and appealing to all people of good will and honest concern, a way that not only expresses their understanding of human behavior, but tests it and helps it to expand. For this reason, they distinguish carefully between religious belief and religious ethics. Religious ethics is the examination of moral situations from a particular religious perspective. In it, the religious doctrine is not a substitute for inquiry. It is a starting point, a guide to inquiry and to organizing the findings of inquiry.

The Need for Ethics

It is foolish to argue that we don't need ethics because we have law and religious belief. It is because of ethics (moral reasoning) that we have law in the first place, and we continue to need ethics to refine and perfect our legal system. We also need ethics in order to discuss the practical implications of our religious belief with others who do not share that belief. In addition, in situations where the reasonableness of a particular article of belief is at issue, we need ethics to help us reach a sound decision.

Two brief examples, both actual cases, will dramatize the need for ethics. The religion known as Voodoo, which originated thousands of years ago in Africa, is still practiced in some parts of the world by as many as 275 million people. It has a number of adherents in the United States, mainly in New York City, Miami, and New Orleans. Most of these adherents are black and Hispanic; some are white. Religious practices of Voodoo, known as Santeria in the United States, no longer include human sacrifice, but they do include animal sacrifice and the casting of spells with the aid of dolls or figurines. In the summer of 1982, a farmer's field in upstate New York was the site of such a ritual. Four Voodoo dolls were found mutilated, and the area was littered with the bloody remains of a number of chickens, pigeons, lambs, and goats. Some of the animals and birds appeared to have had their heads *bitten off*.[2] Since the ritual was religious, it cannot effectively be objected

6

to on religious grounds (except by saying, "My religious views make me deplore that religious practice"). And it may have broken no law, so the only legal objection may be "There *ought to be* a law." But on what basis ought there to be (or not be) a law? On the basis of moral judgment. Ethics.

The second example occurred in Minden, Louisana. Because of their religious belief that God heals illness, a couple sought no medical help for their infant granddaughter, who was suffering from meningitis. When she died, they were arrested and charged with negligent homicide. A jury found them guilty.[3] In this case, the law and religious belief directly clash. If the law were the final arbiter of right and wrong, it would be impossible (or at least pointless) to discuss the case further. Yet we can discuss it further, can dispute whether the law is defensible and whether the decision in this case served justice. Whatever our position may be, it will be a product of ethical judgment.

In addition to this need for ethics, there is another, perhaps even more basic need. Ethics permits us to interpret everyday human actions and to decide what behavior we approve in others and want to emulate ourselves. Is it morally acceptable to copy another person's answer to a homework problem if we've tried unsuccessfully to solve it? Should we lie to the friend who asks our opinion about how his hair looks if we think it looks terrible? Is it ethical to steal something from a roommate who lost something of ours and never offered to replace it? Was the man in the plane crash who kept helping others to safety until he drowned in the icy waters of the Potomac River a hero or a fool? Were those who accepted his help behaving less morally than he? Ethics can help us find satisfying answers to such questions.

Some Preliminary Guidelines

Later chapters will develop the guidelines that are necessary to reach thorough and thoughtful ethical judgments. But you will find it helpful to have a preliminary approach to use in the meantime. The basic problem you will have to deal with is the tendency to prejudge cases. In the case of the "mate-swapping" schoolteacher, we noted how religious belief can lead to prejudgment. The problem, of course, is not limited to believers. A nonbeliever who feels strongly that adultery is morally acceptable but job discrimination because of life-style is reprehensible might approach the issue with his or her mind made up, too. The possibility that the board acted correctly might be inconceivable to this person.

Few people are completely free from the inclination to prejudgment on at least some issues. Some people may have their answer ready for any question concerning war; others, for questions concerning private property; still others, for issues involving alcohol or drugs. And many will have answers ready for questions of sexual morality. The reasons for prejudging will vary—from traumatic experience to personal preference to simple opinion. The underlying attitudes may range from distrust of all regulations, all laws, even all *thoughts,* to an uncritical endorsement of all traditions. But in each case the effect is the same: to avoid thinking about the particular case at all, and merely to call forth a prefabricated, all-purpose answer.

The alternative to the closed mind is not the empty mind, however. Even if we wished to set aside completely all our prior conclusions about human behavior and right and wrong, we could not do so. The mind cannot be manhandled that way. Nor should it be. We can expect, then, that a flood of impressions and reactions will rush in upon our thoughts when we consider a moral issue. It is not the fact of that flood that matters, nor its force. It is what we do to avoid having our judgment swept away by it. Here are some suggestions:

1. *Be aware of your first impressions. Note them carefully.* Knowing the way your thinking inclines is the first step toward balancing it.

2. *Consider other views and the arguments that could be used to support them.* The position that directly opposes your first impression is often the most helpful one to consider. If your impression is wrong, this will help you find out. If it is not, then you can return to it with confidence and present it more effectively for having considered alternatives to it.

3. *Keep your thinking flexible.* Do not feel obligated to your early ideas. The process of ethical thinking entails entertaining many ideas, some of which you will accept, some of which you will discard as inferior. No judgment is your "official" judgment until you endorse it publicly in speaking or writing. So change your mind as often as you like as you analyze an issue. The more fully and un-prejudicially you explore the issue, the better your judgment is likely to be.

4. *Express your judgment precisely and explain the reasoning that underlies it.* It is all too easy to say something you don't quite mean, especially when the issue is both complex and controversial. The best way to avoid this problem is to experiment with several differ-ent ways of expressing your judgment instead of accepting the first version you produce. If your judgment is not a simple "yes" or "no," but a form of "it depends," be sure to specify what it de-pends on and exactly how your judgment would vary in different circumstances. Finally, no *statement* of your judgment is sufficient by itself. Be sure to explain, in as much detail as necessary for understanding, *what line of reasoning leads you to that conclusion rather than some other one.*

As you do the inquiries in this chapter and subsequent chapters, you may find it helpful to look back at these guidelines from time to time, at least until you become familiar with them. If you find that you need more help than they provide, turn to the Appendix and read "Writing About Moral Issues."

INQUIRIES

1 Wiretapping is legal with court authorization. Is it also morally right? Is wiretapping ever morally right without court authorization? Consider these cases.

(a) The police receive a tip that someone is engaged in smuggling marijuana into the United States from Mexico.

(b) The FBI uncovers a plot to assassinate top government officials and take over the government.

(c) A suspicious pro football coach suspects his quarterback of shaving points.

2   A village on the seacoast places restrictions on the use of its beaches. Residents of the village are issued beach passes for themselves and their guests. All others are barred. Is such a restriction a moral issue? That is, is it debatable in terms of right and wrong? Explain.

3   There is no legal obligation for an eligible voter to vote in an election in the United States. Is the decision to vote or not to vote a moral decision? Explain.

4   Certain people have spoken out against the American government's foreign and domestic policies. They have broken no laws. Their protests have been fully within the guarantees of free speech. Yet the FBI is directed to investigate each individual thoroughly. The FBI conducts background studies, including interviews with relatives, friends, and acquaintances. Are these investigations ethically justifiable? Explain.

5   A married couple, both addicted to drugs, are unable to care for their infant daughter. She is taken from them by court order and placed in a foster home. The years pass. She comes to regard her foster parents as her real parents. They love her as they would their own daughter. When the child is nine years old, her natural parents, rehabilitated from drugs, begin court action to regain custody. The case is decided in their favor. The child is returned to them, against her will. Does ethics support the law in this case? Discuss.

6   A sociology professor spots a magazine article that will fit in well with the textbook chapter he has assigned his students. However, copyright law forbids his making copies of it without obtaining the publisher's or author's permission (usually given for a small fee). Since he cannot use college funds for this purpose, and since there isn't sufficient time to go through the process of obtaining permission, he decides to break the law and make the copies. Does he act rightly? Explain.

7   Zoo officials in Eureka, California, could not afford to house two healthy adult bears while a new bear grotto was being built, and the only other zoo that would take the bears was in South Dakota. Since the zoo could not afford the $500 it would have cost to transport the bears, officials decided to destroy them. As their two 3-month-old cubs looked on, the bears were given lethal shots of sodium pheno-barbital.[4] Was the bears' destruction a moral issue? If so, was the action morally wrong?

8   Lawrence Steubig stole six candy bars in 1941. He was judged incompetent to stand trial and was sent to a mental institution. He was freed in 1975, *thirty-four years* later, whereupon he sued officials at the institution for "loss of liberty and loss of enjoyment of life." The institution could produce no records to show that he had ever received therapy or a chance to prove his competency. The judge ruled that Steubig's Fourteenth Amendment rights had been violated, but that he was not entitled to collect damages because the officials of the institution had acted in good faith.[5] Is this verdict defensible on moral grounds?

9   Kenneth A. Goon of Vestal, New York, unwittingly paid sewer bills for more than $1300 over an eighteen-year period and then discovered there was no sewer line connected to his home. Since the statute of limitations on civil suits of this kind is six years, the town attorney suggested that Goon be reimbursed for six years of payments only.[6] Do you find this legal position morally supportable?

10 Federal agents, acting on a tip that $4 million in profits from the sale of heroin was hidden in a roofing contractor's home, obtained a search warrant, entered the home, and proceeded to tear it apart. Walls were torn down, furniture ripped apart, the siding and patio tiles loosened. Trenches were dug in the yard. The toilet bowl was smashed. The "work" went on for almost twenty-four hours and caused an estimated $50,000 damage. The owner, who was married to the sister of a convicted narcotics dealer but had no criminal record, sued for damages. The law, however, was vague on the point. One law professor stated that there was virtually no legal precedent for such a suit. Nor was it clear who should be held responsible. The federal government? The federal agents? Their supervisor? (After the incident, the agents' supervisor said he believed the men had conducted a "reasonable search.")[7] Frame your own answer to these questions from an ethical standpoint.

11 In November 1981, a Milpitas, California, boy raped and then killed his girlfriend and dumped her body in a lovers' lane gulley. Over the next few days, the killer boasted to his high school friends and the word quickly spread that the girl was dead and that her body was in the gulley. Carload after carload of high school students visited the gulley to see the body. Some students prodded it with sticks or kicked it; one girl ripped a decal from the dead girl's jeans. Only one boy reported the murder to the high school principal, and even after the police investigation was well under way, only two students would identify the killer or volunteer any information. Since failure to report a body or to volunteer to testify are not crimes, the students could not be charged legally.[8] But was the behavior of any of the students morally objectionable?

Comparing Cultures

CHAPTER 2

How do we account for the fact that an action that is praised in one culture may be condemned in another? Doesn't this suggest that all moral values are relative to the culture they are found in?

Cultures differ in their ideas about right and wrong, and the differences are not always slight. In more than a few instances, one culture's sin is another's virtue. For example, the conception of marriage that Americans are most familiar with—one wife and one husband joined for life—is not universal. In some cultures serial monogamy—marrying several times—is not merely tolerated (as it is beginning to be in the United States), but is regarded as neutral or even good. And in Siberia, "a Koryak woman . . . would find it hard to understand how a woman could be so selfish and so undesirous of female companionship in the home as to wish to restrict her husband to one mate."[1]

Sex before marriage has been generally viewed as immoral in the West. Yet in some island cultures, it is encouraged. Homosexuals are hounded and tormented as immoral deviants in some cultures; in others they are accepted without reservation.

Such differences are not limited to sexual morality. It is considered a person's moral obligation in some cultures to assist a blood relative in any enterprise, even stealing from others. Certain tribes of headhunters may raid neighboring villages and return with the villagers' heads for no other reason than that their "supply" of names has been used up and before a new name may be claimed, one must possess the head it belonged to.[2] In contrast, among the Tasaday tribe of the Philippines violence is apparently unknown.

It is commonly thought that at least one action—the taking of life—would be unanimously condemned by people of all cultures. Here is

13

what anthropologist Ruth Benedict has to say about that idea in her classic study, *Patterns of Culture:*

> On the contrary, in a matter of homicide, it may be held that one is blameless if diplomatic relations have been severed between neighbouring countries, or that one kills by custom his first two children, or that a husband has right of life and death over his wife, or that it is the duty of the child to kill his parents before they are old. It may be that those are killed who steal a fowl, or who cut their upper teeth first, or who are born on a Wednesday. Among some peoples a person suffers torments at having caused an accidental death; among others it is a matter of no consequence. Suicide also may be a light matter, the recourse of anyone who has suffered some slight rebuff, an act that occurs constantly in a tribe. It may be the highest and noblest act a wise man can perform. The very tale of it, on the other hand, may be a matter for incredulous mirth, and the act itself impossible to conceive as a human possibility. Or it may be a crime punishable by law, or regarded as a sin against the gods.[3]

In *Patterns of Culture*, Benedict details the customs, values, and beliefs of three cultures. One of them is the culture of several groups of Indians of the Northwest Coast of America, mainly the Kwakiutl of Vancouver Island, whose traditional way of life survived until the end of the nineteenth century. Among those tribes it was accepted practice to murder a man to acquire the rights to his name, his special dances, his personal crests and symbols. Similarly, when a loved one died, the mourners would search for someone of equal rank in a neighboring tribe, announce their intention of killing that person, and then proceed to do so. In this way, they bested fate and the pain of sorrow not by reacting passively, but by striking back.[4]

Another interesting culture described by Benedict is that of Dobu Island off the coast of New Guinea. The Dobuans' entire life is spent in vicious competition. The rule of virtually every social enterprise is *cheat your neighbor*. The good man, the respected man, is the one who has succeeded in outfoxing his opponent. The Dobuan who wishes to injure someone, unlike the Northwest Coast Indian, does not announce his plan but pretends affection and does his treachery in secret or by surprise. The sorcery that the Dobuans practice on one another is, in their view, made more potent by closeness to the victim.

An enviable accomplishment of Dobuan life is the successful practice of *wabuwabu*. By it a person victimizes another. He may promise to trade the same valuable possession to several traders or break an engagement for marriage after obtaining the usual property settlement from the father of the betrothed. "It is taken for granted," Benedict notes, "that the Dobuan has thieved, killed children and his close associates by sorcery, cheated whenever he dared."[5]

Interpreting Cultural Differences

What are we to make of such differences among cultures? What conclusions are we to draw? The principle that covers such cases is the principle of cultural relativity. It means that the ingredients of a culture do not depend on any absolutes outside that culture and above all other cultures; instead, they vary according to the background and development and natural habitat of the particular culture. By "ingredients" we mean all important matters of the culture's life: social customs, religious rituals, mythology, attitudes toward nature and other peoples.

In the largest sense the principle of cultural relativity is too obvious to be disputed; yet it is controversial because it has been subject to divergent interpretations. The basis of the controversy is not so much the principle itself as the conclusions that some leap to from the principle. The most common conclusion* is that "If there is no observable control transcending all cultures, no eternal book of rules, then right and wrong are a matter of opinion and it doesn't matter what we do: *anything goes!*" This conclusion does not, however, necessarily follow from the principle. Some authorities, in fact, declare that this conclusion is decidedly what cultural relativity does *not* mean.

"The principle of cultural relativity," anthropologist Clyde Kluckhohn writes, "does not mean that because the members of some savage tribe are allowed to behave in a certain way that this fact gives intellectual warrant for such behavior in all groups. Cultural relativity means, on the contrary, that the appropriateness of any positive or

*Another common conclusion is discussed in Chapter 3.

negative custom must be evaluated with regard to how this habit fits with other group habits."[6]

In their studies of various cultures, modern anthropologists have found that it is all too easy to misinterpret people's behavior. What seems to be so may not really be so. Just as it is natural for us to evaluate the behavior of others by our own standards, so is it natural to view actions in other cultures from the perspective of the codes of our own culture. What seems fair to us we assume is fair to other people; and when we see an action that we consider treacherous, we assume that by that action they have violated their own code. Yet deeper understanding may reveal that individuals in the other culture have not only not been violating their code but have in fact been observing it.

The only way to penetrate the deception of appearance is to study the cultural context in which an action occurs, determining the circumstances of time, place, and condition surrounding it and, most important, learning the reasoning that underlies it and the moral value it reflects.

Kluckhohn cites an example from World War II. The behavior of some Japanese captives confounded American military men. On occasion, Japanese who had demonstrated fanatical allegiance to their emperor by risking their lives in suicide missions would, after being captured, write propaganda for the Americans, reveal information about Japanese bases, and even fly reconnaisance missions against their own people. To many American servicemen such behavior must have seemed cowardly and immoral. Yet to anthropologists familiar with the Japanese ethical system, Kluckhohn notes, the behavior was not mysterious at all. Japanese morality was *situational*. In the situation where they were fighting in the service of the emperor, their moral code bid them serve him unquestioningly. But in the situation of capture, that same moral code bid them transfer their allegiance to the new authority, their captors.[7]

The strangeness of ways of thinking and acting that are foreign to us can lead us to overemphasize the differences among cultures. New and unfamiliar things always have a certain dramatic impact. The exciting details of anthropological studies make it tempting to reason that, if the morality of actions is so widely different, then the underlying values the actions are based on must also be radically different. In some cases they are. According to the Dobuan's view of life, as we have seen, "virtue consists in selecting a victim upon whom he can vent the malignancy he attributes alike to human society and to the powers of nature."[8]

The Similarity of Values

The Dobuan's culture is, in that respect, quite atypical, and in other cultures the differences in values are more apparent than real. Sometimes a difference in behavior is attributable to a *different way of viewing the same value*, as in the case of the Japanese prisoners of war. At other times it is attributable to *the observance of a religious belief or taboo*, as in the case of a Hindu's refusal to kill a sacred cow to provide food for starving people. At still other times it reflects *the belief that some other, higher value takes precedence*. The Northwest Coast Indian's practice of taking a life to balance the death of a loved one is an example. The reason for the action is not a lack of a sense of fairness toward the victim, but that heroic retaliation against life's tragedies is a prior obligation.

Even in cases where none of the foregoing explanations applies, a value may, because of a people's behavior, appear absent but actually be present. In such cases, *the value is simply not considered applicable to the victims.* Consider two cases discussed earlier in the chapter: the man who helped his relative steal and the headhunters who replenished their supply of names. Although we may judge that they were acting without a sense of justice or fairness, both were in fact acting on the idea that *outsiders*, those alien to family or tribe, are "beyond the pale of moral consideration."[9] Justice and fairness are seen as not covering them. They are not persons; hence they have no rights. (If such reasoning seems bizarre, remember that many American slave-owners had similar attitudes toward their slaves, and that the domestic and foreign policies of "civilized" countries do not always, even to this day, coincide.)

The conclusion that even these few cases suggest is that rules of

17

behavior may vary greatly from culture to culture, but the underlying values are usually similar, often remarkably so. There is justice and courage, respect for one's relatives and tribesmen, subordination of individual whim to custom or the judgments of tribal sages. If it is a mistake to deny the differences in human values, such as the aberrant Dobuan culture represents, then surely it is an even greater mistake to deny the similarities.

INQUIRIES

In each of the following cases, the behavior illustrated seems to suggest that the people's values differ significantly from our own. Consider the possibility that, beneath appearances, the values are similar. Develop a plausible explanation for the difference in behavior.

1   In one culture, the elderly and those with severe handicaps are put to death. It would appear that this culture does not recognize human dignity as a value.

2   In another culture, this habit is observed: A person will ask a relative to do a task that requires days of labor and, when it is completed, never even thank the relative. On the other hand, if a stranger renders anyone the slightest service, the stranger is lavishly rewarded. It would appear that a sense of fairness is lacking in this culture.

3   A common practice of a tribe living in a remote jungle area is to shun the sick. The moment members of the tribe become seriously ill, they cease to exist in the tribe's view. They must leave the village and care for themselves. If they recover, however, they are restored to tribal membership. Apparently, the tribe lacks compassion for the afflicted.

4   A group of young boys are gathered together. Several men approach them, brandishing sticks and whips. They beat the boys viciously. The other male members of the tribe sit by and watch, laughing and obviously enjoying the event. It would seem that the men of this culture are sadistic, deriving pleasure from seeing others in pain.

5   Whenever hunters in a certain culture are asked how their day's hunting went, they say "very well" and go on to declare that their relatives and friends and ancestors will be pleased with them. They say this whether they return heavily laden or empty-handed. It appears that truth-telling has no value in this culture.

6   One woman finds another eating a piece of wild fruit. She calls to her neighbors and they stone the offender to death. Since the punishment does not fit the crime, it would appear that this culture lacks a sense of proportion and fails to recognize the value of human life.

7   In an island culture, the men are seen returning from a fishing expedition. One man runs his canoe happily up on the beach. The villagers cheer him. Then a second canoe arrives. The second fisherman leaps out, runs to the first man, seizes his basket of fish, and throws it into the sea. He goes unpunished. The tribe seems to tolerate stealing.

8   In some technologically advanced cultures, young people are "tracked" early in life to certain vocations and training programs. As adults, they have few career options and are expected to follow a path chosen for them. Apparently, the culture does not value self-determination and individual well-being.

Judging Issues

CHAPTER 3

*Doesn't the fact of such great differences in basic
ethical judgments (if not in underlying values)
among cultures caution us against claiming that
any culture is better than others? Isn't it a mark of
ignorance to pass judgment on the morality of
those who disagree with us?*

The phrasing chosen for the above questions is deliberate. It
matches the phrasing commonly used in expressing the widespread view that it is improper to judge the moral codes of other cultures. The problem with such phrasing, however, is that it is ambiguous
in two ways. What does "better than" mean? And precisely what kind
of "judgment" is referred to?

"Better than" is obviously a term of comparison. It has many variations: People speak of cultures being "higher than" others, or "surpass-
ing" them. But whenever someone makes this kind of comparison—
"The Egyptian culture was better than the Roman" or "Our culture has
surpassed all others"—the sensitive person cringes, for such statements
have one of two implications. The first is that the "higher" culture has
outdistanced the other in every particular of language, custom, behavior, learning, artistic achievement, and material accomplishment.
Such a performance may be theoretically possible, but it is quite improb-
able. Proclaiming it casually, without documentation, invites disbelief.
The other possible implication is that one culture has bested the other in
some overall tally in which virtues are added and vices subtracted. And
that is ludicrous.

Thus "better than" comparisons are rightly seen as presumptuous.
It is understandable that because of them many are led to reject all
comparisons of cultures, to suspend evaluation. But that is a mistake.

What is wrong with "better than" comparisons is not that they dare to make value judgments about cultures, but that they do so in a loose, sweeping manner, and without specifying exactly what is being judged.

It is possible to make *reasonable* value judgments about other cultures. Consider this value judgment: "Culture A has achieved a less violent attitude toward its neighbors than culture B has." Assuming that the facts in the case supported the judgment—culture A has never attacked another country whereas culture B has a history of military aggression, culture A's approach to international disputes is always conciliatory whereas culture B's is usually threatening, and so on—the judgment would be indisputable. Consider another value judgment: "In sharp contrast to culture C, culture D practices admirable tolerance of homosexuals." If the facts, acknowledged by expert observers of the cultures, demonstrated that culture C denies homosexuals access to jobs, to housing, and to higher education, while culture D treats them no differently from heterosexuals, there would be no basis for objecting to (or for resisting) the judgment.

If reasonable value judgments about other cultures are possible, why do some people resist all such judgments? To understand their thinking, let's return for a moment to the discussion of cultural relativity that we began in the previous chapter. There we noted that the principle of relativity (that people's values reflect their culture) is too obvious to be disputed, but that some people leap from that principle to erroneous conclusions. The most common erroneous conclusion, which we examined, is that "anything goes" in human conduct.

Now let's examine another common conclusion that people leap to from the same principle of relativity. That conclusion is "Whatever a culture affirms to be right or wrong is by that fact right or wrong for everyone in that culture." Once people have accepted this idea, it is easy for them to reason as follows: "We disapprove of headhunting, but the Wugabuga tribe approves of it, so it is wrong for us but right for them."

Such thinking seems very democratic. It demonstrates charity, humility, a live-and-let-live generosity. Unfortunately, it sits on the brink of absurdity. When we examine it critically, we are prompted to respond, "Right for them but wrong for us? No, that's nonsense. Despite the fact that our cultures differ, despite the fact that the Wugabuga's headhunting is perfectly understandable given their history, geography, and world view, headhunting is not justifiable. It is an invasion of the basic rights of the victims. Admittedly, the Wugabuga do not acknowledge those rights. But they *should*. And given further development and increased contact with other peoples, they surely will recognize the need to do so."

Understanding Versus Justification

The distinction between *understanding* and *justification* is a crucial one. As human beings, imperfect in our grasp of reality, necessarily groping toward our answers, we must constantly reach out to others and strive to understand their views. To be closed to others' views and the reasoning that leads to them, to judge these matters in ignorance, or in the twilight of fragmentary knowledge, is to stunt our growth as human beings. Yet explanation is not justification. The ancient Spartans had a very logical reason for whipping young boys viciously. It was a ritual that marked their introduction into manhood and symbolized the physical toughness required of the citizens of a warrior state. But that reason doesn't make the action right.

Similarly, we can thoroughly understand the thinking of slave traders without approving their occupation. We can gain deep psychological insights into the Nazi persecution of the Jews—indeed, insights that the Nazis themselves could not grasp—and yet condemn their program of extermination as utterly wrong.

Judgment Is Unavoidable

The behavior of other cultures in certain situations sheds light on our behavior in similar situations. For example, in ancient Persia and Egypt criminals were not only used in medical experiments; they were treated more like laboratory animals than human beings. In the eighteenth century, the Princess of Wales had six condemned criminals and six poor children vaccinated against smallpox to determine whether the vaccine would be safe for her children. Had the criminals and poor children died (in her view, before any real harm was done), she would have decided not to vaccinate her own children. Early in this century, at Harvard a professor of medicine infected some criminals with plague, allegedly without their consent, as an experiment.[1]

Did the Harvard professor act ethically? Whatever our answer, we probably have no qualms about answering. But dare we evaluate a case in eighteenth-century England? Should we presume to pass judgment on the case in ancient Persia and Egypt? Yes. *We cannot help but do so.* In all three cases we are dealing with essentially the same situation. Even though circumstances alter cases and we could judge each differently, any judgment that we made of one would have implications for the others.

This is not to say that judgments of other cultures should be made casually. On the contrary, they should be made carefully and tentatively. The attitude that should permeate all our inquiry into other cultures is that every culture is of human design and therefore no culture (including our own) is perfect, that every culture has its areas of moral sensitivity and insensitivity. Each has its own portion of wisdom and of ignorance. Each has much to learn from the others.

Neither does the fact that judgment is unavoidable mean that we should necessarily *express* our view and try to persuade people of another culture that their view is wrong. There may be occasions when the seriousness of the situation leaves us no choice but to speak out. Those occasions, however, are rare. Unless there is a compelling need to speak out, or we are specifically asked to share our views, we should refrain from expressing our judgment of another culture to members of that culture.

The rest of this book could easily be spent comparing the ethical tradition we have inherited with the ethical traditions of other cultures. That would be a fascinating study and an instructive one. But it would demand a thorough examination of all cultures, including our own, in times past as well as time present. Little opportunity would remain for learning the skills of ethical analysis and judgment and for addressing

23

the rich assortment of issues that confront us today. For this reason we will not pursue comparisons with other cultures in any formal way. Occasionally we will consider issues that involve another culture. (The speed of modern travel and the high technology we enjoy in communication have multiplied our interactions with other cultures and raised some interesting ethical questions.) However, our principal focus will be on making ethical judgments within our culture.

Issues in Our Culture

The judgment of issues within our own culture is easier in the sense that it does not require learning about another people and a different value system. But it is more difficult in that it demands that we look objectively at ideas and beliefs to which we have developed strong emotional attachments. We can take nothing for granted, not even our attitude toward our culture, because that attitude can influence the way we analyze issues. If, for example, we are alienated from our culture and reject its moral perspective, we will be inclined to overlook its virtues. On the other hand if, as is more likely, we accept its perspective consciously or unconsciously, we will be inclined to overlook its shortcomings. In addition, when we share our culture's perspective, one crippling assumption is liable to run through all our evaluations: Its view is right because it is familiar to us and we feel comfortable with it or because it is modern. Neither familiarity or modernity is a valid measure of an idea.

Another problem in dealing with contemporary issues in our own culture is the special reluctance we feel about examining issues close to our everyday lives. Judging the actions of the experimenting Harvard professor of more than fifty years ago, or those of the slaveowner of an earlier time, poses little difficulty. But when the actions are those of our relatives and friends, our teachers and roommates, the writers and media "personalities" we revere, we feel obliged to forgo moral judgment. The same democratic spirit we feel toward the Wugabuga tribe, we feel even more intensely toward our own tribe. "To each his own," we say. "Who am I to judge?"

24

The kinds of moral issues we must deal with today add to our tendency to respond this way. The issues are controversial, perplexing, sometimes without precedent. The very mention of abortion triggers strong sentiments. The question of what weapons are legitimate in a war of defense is fraught with complexity. The issues of genetic engineering and chemical stimulation of the brain pose new dilemmas.

Yet even though the urge to say "It's wrong to judge" is understandable, it is just as mistaken a response within a culture as it is among cultures. Judging an action is not the same as judging the person who performs it. "Love me, love my idea" is not a reasonable demand; and mature people know better than to make it. We can disagree with the conclusions of others without straining mutual respect and friendship because, though courtesy is a civilized requirement for dealing with other people, it does not extend to ideas.

It is true, of course, that judgment of others' views involves not only the risk of error, but also the risk of offending others. However, the alternative is to evade judgment when judgment is needed, and that is unworthy of thinking creatures; or to feign approval where we secretly disapprove, and that is deceitful.

INQUIRIES

1   The Eskimo husband's sense of hospitality requires him to offer his wife to an overnight guest. In our culture this is considered wrong. Is one view more justifiable than the other? Explain your reasoning carefully.

2   The case of the Japanese fliers detailed in Chapter 2 reveals a different view of allegiance to authority than we are accustomed to. If American fliers were captured by the Japanese, we would have expected them to retain their loyalty to the United States rather than transfer it to their captors. Is one of these views more justifiable? Explain.

3 In some ancient cultures a young maiden was sacrificed each year to ensure a good harvest. In others, when the king died, many servants were killed and buried with him so that his needs in the afterlife could be suitably attended. Such practices are understandable, given the beliefs of the people. Are they morally right? Why or why not?

4 In ancient Rome, Sparta, and China defective children and unwanted children were abandoned to die. Comment on the morality of this practice.

5 In some cultures a person who kills someone by accident must support the victim's family thereafter. In our culture we expect life insurance and social security to cover the family's needs. If the one responsible for the accident is found to be legally blameless, he or she is customarily considered morally blameless as well. Compare and evaluate these moral views.

6 Review the Dobuan moral code and underlying view of life presented in Chapter 2. To what extent is the code ethically justifiable?

7 A Christian missionary is sent to preach the Gospel to members of a newly discovered tribe. After arriving in their primitive jungle settlement and establishing a friendly relationship with them, she learns that they encourage extramarital promiscuity. She believes that this is morally wrong. She therefore explains to them that such promiscuity is immoral, an offense against God. Is the missionary's action ethical?

8 The same Christian missionary next learns that once each year, as an inducement to the god of the hunt to smile upon their efforts, members of the tribe cut off someone's right hand. (Whose right hand is determined quite democratically, by lottery.) The missionary is appalled by this custom and explains to the tribe that it is based on pure superstition. Is the missionary's action justifiable?

9 The missionary now makes an even more startling discovery. Since tribe members believe women are inferior to men and a tribe with a large number of women is an outrage to the god of good sense, they strictly control the female population. Whenever the number of girl babies exceeds the percentage approved by the wise men of the tribe, they permit no more girl babies born that year to live. More specifically, they take newborn babies out into the wilderness to die. The missionary tries to persuade them that such behavior is wrong. Is this action justifiable? Does your answer to this question agree with your answers to the first two questions? If not, explain why.

The Role of the Majority View

CHAPTER 4

Is the basis for deciding moral values within a culture the majority view? In other words, if the majority of the citizens of our country should decide that a particular action is right, would that very decision make the action right?

We live in an age when statistics confront us at every turn. From the moment we arise, we are bombarded by authoritative voices thrusting percentages at us. "Sixty-seven point two percent of the American public support the President's tax program." "Seven out of ten doctors recommend No-Ouch tablets." "My group had 90 percent less underarm odor." It is therefore not surprising that we often think that more is better; if the majority agree that something is so, then it must be so.

But what, after all, is the "majority"? It is nothing more than 51 percent or more of the *individuals* in a group. Although the conversion of a bunch of individual views into a statistic can create the impression of authoritativeness and wisdom, those qualities do not always result. *There is no magic in majorities.*

If we were to examine a particular majority and compare their individual thinking on a particular issue, what would we find? First, we would find that actual knowledge of the issue varied widely among the individuals. Some would be well informed about all details. Others would be completely uninformed, yet unaware of their ignorance. Between these extremes would be the largest group: those partly informed and partly ignorant, in some ways perceptive but in other ways confused or mistaken.

Second, we would find significant variations in the degree and

28

quality of consideration given the facts. Some individuals would have read or listened to the views of authorities, sorted out irrelevancies, appraised each authority's position in light of available evidence, and weighed all possibile interpretations of the facts. Others would have taken the ultimate shortcut and forgone all inquiry on the assumption that their intuition is infallible. A large middle group would have made some inquiry, but less than exhaustive and sometimes less than adequate.

Finally, we would find wide differences in the quality of judgment of the issue. Some would have judged quite objectively, avoiding preconceived notions and prejudices, and being critical of all views, including those to which they are naturally disposed. Others would have been ruled completely by emotion, untempered by reason, their judgment little more than a conditioned reflex. Again, most would have achieved some middle position in which thought and "gut reaction" intermingled to produce more or less objective conclusions.

A Sample Situation

To see how all these differences might work in an actual moral issue, let's take the question "Is it wrong to kill enemy civilians in time of war?" Imagine that we have asked this question of a representative sampling of the general public and that a slender majority has answered in the negative. What variations in knowledge, inquiry, and judgment would the statistical report cover? What actual lines of thought might have occurred to the individuals in the majority? Here are some probabilities.

> Mr. A: "If they started the war, then the blame would be on them and they'd deserve no mercy. They'd all be responsible for their government's actions; so all of them, civilians and soldiers alike, would be regarded as enemies. If they get hurt, that's the breaks."
> Mr. B: "I fought in Vietnam and, believe me, in that war you couldn't tell a friend from an enemy. I've seen children waving and shouting greetings as they approached with explosives attached to their backs. I've seen peasants who'd shoot you in the back or direct you into a mine field after you'd given them candy. It can't be wrong to kill civilians in war because it's necessary for survival."

29

Ms. C: "No, it's not wrong if it helps to shorten the war. In World War II we avoided more deaths and injuries to our armed forces and brought them home sooner by dropping atom bombs on two Japanese cities. Many civilians were in those cities. But our main intention was not to kill civilians; it was to end the war. Therefore the bombing was justified."

Ms. D: "It's a complex question. It really depends on the circumstances. The bombings of Dresden, Hiroshima, and Nagasaki during World War II were very wrong in my view. Those targets were selected *because* they were population centers and their destruction would demoralize the enemy. In other words, civilians were deliberately singled out for elimination. No goal, however worthy, justifies such slaughter. On the other hand, in a guerrilla war, the distinction between combatant and noncombatant is somewhat blurred. Soldiers disguise themselves as civilians. And civilians are enlisted, sometimes against their will, to perform military acts. In such a war I can conceive of situations where the killing of civilians is justified; say, where a soldier is in doubt whether the civilian approaching him is armed and must choose to shoot or jeopardize his own life. Is it wrong to kill civilians? I'd have to say no, not necessarily."

Perhaps none of these views is the best one possible, but the last one is much more penetrating than the others. It shows a willingness to consider the differences, as well as the similarities, between particular acts of war. It reveals sensitivity to important distinctions—specifically, to the distinction between the circumstances of the World War II bombings and the conditions of a guerrilla war. Finally, it demonstrates an awareness of the dilemma faced by particular people who must make a moral decision in actual war situations, the kill-or-be-killed choice that must be made instantly, without time for careful reflection.

Although Ms. D's view is a much better response than the others, in a statistical report its excellence would be ignored. It would merely be lumped with the others, including the utterly shallow and morally insensitive view of Mr. A. In statistical computation, "yes" or "no" is everything. The depth or shallowness of the thought that supports the answer counts for nothing. (It is possible, of course, for statistical reports to include the full answers, but even when a report is set up to provide for such answers, which it seldom is, the need for brevity often forces their omission.)

The Majority Can Err

In short, the majority view is less than perfect. To assume that it is necessarily enlightened is a serious mistake. If 1 percent or 49 percent of the population can be shallow or prejudiced in their view of an issue, so can 51 or 99 percent. Corporate ignorance is as common as corporate wisdom.

At various times in history the majority have supported outrageous deeds. In some ancient societies the majority believed in and practiced murdering female babies, abandoning crippled infants to die, murdering young men and women as sacrifices to the gods or to serve a deceased monarch in the afterlife. The majority have supported religious wars, child labor, even child prostitution. In Hitler's Germany the majority gave at least silent assent to the persecution of the Jews. For centuries the standard treatment of the mentally ill, universally accepted, bordered on torture. Until recently in the southern United States racial intermarriage was not only morally condemned but legally prohibited.

If the majority view determined right and wrong, then slavery was not wrong when it was practiced in America. It was right as long as the majority accepted it and became wrong only when more than 50 percent of the people rejected it. If the majority's moral perspective cannot err, then the religious persecutions that drove the early colonists to this continent were not wrong, were not vices at all, but virtues. Such a view, of course, is nonsense. Slavery and religious persecution would be no less immoral if every country in the world approved them. There must be more to right and wrong than a showing of hands.

To be sure, the majority view may be the only one a democratic society can follow in its procedures of representative government. And even in lawmaking, the majority view will rightly exert considerable influence on legislators (though the true statesman will not hesitate to go against the majority when she or he judges it in their interest to do so). But even in these necessary nods to the majority, there is no guarantee of correctness. The future of the country hangs precariously on the hope that, in urgent matters, the counsel of the majority will be the counsel of wisdom.

31

Yet in ethical judgment, where there is a singular potential for irrational reaction, and even self-deception, it is especially important to avoid slavishly following the majority view. We do well to remember that, just as we view certain practices of past centuries as morally indefensible, so later generations may judge some of our practices similarly. Every age has its blindness, perhaps even its barbarism.

INQUIRIES

Several of the following inquiries involve specific historical events. If you need to know more about those events before making a judgment, you may wish to consult a good encyclopedia or the *New York Times Index.*

1 A 1981 Gallup poll revealed that two-thirds of the American people believe that persons convicted of murder should be sentenced to death.[1] Is the majority right in this case? Is capital punishment ethically justifiable?

2 For centuries it was the common belief among Europeans that it is morally obligatory for society to deny Jews the rights of gentiles. That belief resulted in the segregation of Jews in ghettos, the strict regulation of their marriages, the imposition of special codes of dress on Jewish women, forced attendance at Christian religious ceremonies, and exclusion from certain occupations, including law, medicine, and education. Was that majority view ethically defensible?

3 After the Japanese attack on Pearl Harbor, President Roosevelt ordered the internment of thousands of American citizens of Japanese ancestry. (They were guilty of no crime but were considered *potentially* disloyal because of their ancestry.) A large number of Americans, possibly a majority, supported the president's action on moral grounds. Was the internment morally justifiable?

4   At the turn of this century a majority of lawmakers considered it morally correct to deny women the right to vote. Was that view morally defensible?

5   The dropping of atomic bombs on Hiroshima and Nagasaki in World War II was regarded by millions of Americans, perhaps a majority, as a morally acceptable act. Was the dropping of those bombs morally acceptable?

6   In 1971, after a military court found Lt. William Calley guilty of the premeditated murder of twenty-two unarmed civilians in the Vietnam village of My Lai and sentenced him to dismissal from the army, forfeiture of pay and privileges, and life imprisonment, a national poll revealed that 79 percent of the American public disapproved of the verdict and punishment, presumably on moral grounds.[2] Were the verdict and punishment ethically justifiable?

7   Two years after the U.S. Supreme Court's famous school desegregation order, a national poll revealed that 80 percent of the citizens of southern states opposed school desegregation. The same poll disclosed that 76 percent disapproved of the Interstate Commerce Commission's order banning train, bus, and waiting room segregation.[3] Are such desegregation orders ethically valid?

8   At various times polls have indicated that a majority of Americans favor the outlawing of the Communist Party. Is it ethically valid in a democracy to outlaw any political party that citizens might in good conscience choose to support?

9   A 16-year-old girl visits a birth control clinic and asks to be put on the pill. Since she is a minor, the clinic doctor who writes the prescription for her notifies her parents of the action. Possibly a majority of Americans would approve of the doctor's action. Is the action ethical?

10   In some parts of the country a majority of the citizens pre-

33

sumably believe that it is morally acceptable to send people to jail for smoking marijuana. Is that view correct?

11 Advancements in high technology may eliminate many jobs, particularly for the unskilled worker. The majority of labor union members believe that machines should not replace human workers. Is it ethically justifiable for a society to pursue a course of technological advancement that could leave thousands of workers without jobs?

The Role of Feelings

CHAPTER 5

If the majority view does not determine the rightness of an action, should each person decide on the basis of her or his own feelings, desires, preferences?

The idea of everyone's deciding moral issues on the basis of her or his own feelings, desires, or preferences enjoys some popularity today. "Everyone doing her or his own thing" may seem to be a very reasonable and tolerant approach to morality. It has an understandable appeal to young people who are inclined to challenge their parents' moral code and to those of all ages who are disenchanted with traditional views. It also harmonizes well with the prevailing concern with individuality. If each person is an individual, different from all others, then each person's morality, it would seem, should, like fingerprints, reflect his or her uniqueness.

Those who take this view emphasize making one's life-style and moral perspective reflect one's own needs and wants rather than some prefabricated set of principles that "society" sanctions. They value subjective validity more highly than external norms.

The conclusion that follows from this reasoning is that no one person's view is preferable to another's. Each is good in its own way. One person's religious ritual may be the next person's cardinal sin. Thus if a man and a woman want to marry, that's fine (the same for a man and a man, a woman and a woman). If a couple choose to live together without marrying, that's fine, too. Indeed, if twenty-two people want to live together in multiple liaison, that is also fine. No one other than the individuals themselves has any right to concern himself or herself about it. Freedom is the byword; rules and restrictions are the only heresies.

Now the first thing to notice about this perspective on morality is that it is not very new. Two centuries ago Jean Jacques Rousseau wrote, "What I feel is right is right, what I feel is wrong is wrong." His idea about the relationship of the individual to society underlies the modern perspective. The individual, in Rousseau's view, is inherently good; it is society with its artificial constraints that corrupts the individual. All the modern prompting to "rid ourselves of all inhibitions" and, in more colloquial form, "let it all hang out" have a kinship with Rousseau's thought.

There is no question, of course, that a concern for individuality is legitimate. There do seem to be strong forces at work in the best and freest of human societies that, when unchecked, stifle the uniqueness of persons, promote conformity, and lead to artistic, intellectual, and social sterility. At times rebellion against the prevailing moral views of society is of benefit not only to the individual but to society itself.

Saint Francis shocked the moral sensibilities of his time by giving up the wealth and comfort of his upper-middle-class life to embrace a life of poverty. Many respected people, inclucing his own father, denounced him as shiftless and irresponsible. Yet by persevering in his "madness," he gave the world a luminous example of how to live in imitation of Christ and changed the whole moral focus of his time. Albert Schweitzer incurred the moral indignation of many by choosing to serve the natives in the African jungle rather than continuing to exercise his scholarly and artistic gifts. Yet today his life is regarded as a model of service to humanity. Society judged both men crazy. Society was wrong.

Some Feelings Are Wrong

Countless other examples like Saint Francis and Schweitzer might be cited to show that the feelings, desires, and preferences of certain men and women are wiser than the prevailing wisdom. Yet we still cannot declare that everyone's feelings, desires, and preferences are unassailable. If they were, then we would have no basis for denouncing tyrants, no rationale for condemning the actions of psychopaths, for not only does every great person and every saint go against society's rules, but so does every mugger, every murderer, every child molester.

Hitler presumably was following his feelings and expressing his deepest desires when he exterminated more than six million Jews. Stalin presumably was exercising his preference when he massacred several million peasants. The common spiritual ancestor of both, Genghis Khan, must have achieved emotional satisfaction as he led his hordes across Asia and into Europe, plundering, raping, and devastating. In our own day Charles Manson was following his feelings when he directed his ghoulish followers in their bloodbaths. In each case, these individuals were "doing their thing."

Some years ago in Nassau County, New York, a group of homosexual men were found to be seducing boys as young as 7 years of age. Most of the boys were fatherless. They were recruited with gifts. If they threatened to report the "club" to law enforcement authorities, they, in turn, were threatened with beatings and even death. The adults, of course, were not only feeding their desires, but doing so in an enterprising way.[1]

If no individual's view were better than any other's, if everything were a matter of individual preference, then we would have no choice but to *approve* the actions of all these people. Yet no responsible person would think of approving them. Genocide and ritual murder and the sexual abuse of children are moral outrages.

A Better Guide Is Needed

When we are thinking clearly and being honest with ourselves, we realize that there is a potential in each of us for noble actions of high purpose and honor; but there is also a potential for great mischief and wickedness. Each of us is capable of a wide range of deeds, some that we would be proud if the whole world knew, and others that, if discovered by a single other person, would cause us shame.

A man passing a department store late at night may have a sudden urge to smash the window and steal the cashmere sports jacket he lusts after. A student may feel like spreading a lie about her roommate to avenge a real or imagined wrong. A bank employee may have the desire and even a plan to embezzle a million dollars and depart for the

37

South Seas. Each of us, however placid our nature, may on occasion experience an overwhelming urge to punch someone in the nose. Yet each of these actions is at least of questionable rightness, *despite* the feelings and desires of the person involved.

Similarly, a person walking alone on the shore of a lake may prefer to ignore the call for help that comes from the water. A surgeon relaxing at home may prefer not to answer the call to perform emergency surgery. The father who promised to take his children on a picnic may prefer to play golf with his friends. A lawyer may prefer not to spend the necessary time preparing for the defense of her client. In such situations the answer "whatever the person prefers to do is right to do" is hollow. Good sense suggests that the right action may be at odds with the individual's preference.

Ironically, morality by feelings *completely ignores other people's feelings*. Those who are acted against surely have feelings, too; in the cases cited above their feelings presumably run counter to those committing the actions. If the millions murdered by Hitler and Stalin had been consulted, they surely would have expressed a preference not to be murdered. Similarly, few people enjoy being robbed, lied about, assaulted, or neglected in their time of need. To say that we should be free to do as we wish without regard for others is to say that others should be free to do as they wish without regard for us.* If such a rule were followed, the result would be social chaos.

Since our feelings, desires, and preferences can be either beneficial or harmful, noble or ignoble, praiseworthy or damnable, and since they can be either in harmony or in conflict with other people's feelings, desires, and preferences, they are obviously not accurate tools for analysis of moral issues or trustworthy guidelines to action. Feelings, desires, and preferences need to be evaluated and judged. They need to be measured against some *impartial* standard that will reveal their quality. To make them the basis of our moral decisions is to ignore those needs and to accept them uncritically as the measure of their own worth.

*The argument that people may do whatever they desire to do "as long as no one else is hurt" may seem related, but it is really quite different. It has a social dimension (consideration for others) in addition to a personal dimension (what one wants to do). For this reason we will postpone discussing this argument until a later chapter.

INQUIRIES

1 A Little League baseball coach anticipates a poor season because he lacks a competent pitcher. Just before the season begins, a new family moves into his neighborhood. The coach discovers that one of the boys in the family is an excellent pitcher, but that he is over the age limit for Little League participation. Because the family is not known in the area, the coach is sure he can use the boy without being discovered. He wants a winning season very much, for himself and for his team. Is he morally justified in using the boy?

2 Ralph, a college student, borrows his roommate's car to drive to his aunt's funeral. On the way back he falls asleep at the wheel, veers off the road, and rolls down an embankment. Though he emerges unhurt, the car is a total wreck. Since the car is five years old, the roommate has no collision insurance. Ralph is sorry about the accident but feels no responsibility for paying his roommate what the car was worth. Does he have any moral responsibility to do so?

3 The owner of a roadside restaurant prefers not to serve black customers. She paid for the property, she reasons, and has spent many years developing the business; therefore, she should have the right to decide whom she serves. Is her white-only preference ethically defensible?

4 A small city has a zoning ordinance. The spirit of that ordinance clearly prohibits the operating of a business in areas designated "residential." However, the wording is such that a loophole exists. One woman wishes to open a pet shop in the basement of her split-level home. The law is in her favor. Is morality?

5 The executives of three large appliance companies get together to discuss their competitive situation. Among them they account for 91 percent of the U.S. production of their particular products. They decide that by stabilizing their prices, they can benefit their stockholders, invest more money in product research, and thereby deliver a better product to the consumer. They agree to consult one another before setting prices and to price comparable models at the same price. Is this action ethically acceptable?

6 A man buys a house and later realizes he has paid too much money for it. In fact, he has been badly cheated. There is a bad leak in the cellar and through one wall, the furnace is not functioning properly, and the well is dry at certain times during the year. The cost of putting these things right will be prohibitive. He wants to "unload" the house as soon as possible, and he prefers to increase his chances of recovering his investment by concealing the truth about the house's condition. It is right for him to do so?

7 For over half a century a funeral home in Charlotte, North Carolina, displayed an embalmed human body in a glass showcase. The body was that of a carnival worker who was killed in a fight in 1911. The man's father, also a carnival worker, paid part of the funeral costs and asked the funeral home director to keep the body until he returned. Nothing more was heard from him. Thus the body, clad only in a loincloth, remained on display for sixty-one years. Public clamor finally resulted in its removal from public view. The funeral home director, however (the son of the original director), allegedly felt nothing was wrong in exhibiting the body, which he compared to a mummy in a museum.[2] Is his feeling ethically sound?

8 A newspaper columnist signs a contract with a newspaper chain. Several months later she is offered a position with another newspaper chain at a higher salary. Because she would prefer making more money, she notifies the first chain that she is breaking her contract. The courts will decide the legality of her action. But what of the morality? Did the columnist behave ethically?

9 A California businessman started a check-cashing service, operating out of a large commercial van. He charges customers 1½ percent of the face value of the check for the service, and he has plenty of customers, mainly people on unemployment, welfare, social security, and disability, who lack the bank accounts and credit ratings necessary to cash their checks in a bank. His profit is estimated at almost $50,000 per year. He feels there is nothing unethical about his business.[3] Do you agree?

10 In Mineola, New York, a police officer allegedly posed as a clinical psychologist during his off-duty hours and made phone calls to numerous women inquiring about their sex lives.[4] Presumably he felt that his desire to adopt the pose and make the calls was sufficient to justify his doing so. Do you agree with him?

11 A 16-year-old girl and her father were arrested in Panama City, Florida, for allegedly trying to sell the girl's unborn baby for $500 and a ten-year-old car.[5] Although selling babies is against the law, the two presumably felt that they had the moral right to do so. Is their feeling morally defensible?

12 Two workers were displaced when a company installed a robot to deliver tools and materials to workers in the plant. The robot followed a specially painted track on the plant floor. Several other workers, fearing that their jobs would also be lost, decided to "teach the company a lesson." They repainted the track so that the robot walked off the loading dock and suffered major damage. The workers felt they were justified in their action. Is this an ethically defensible position?

13 An office worker had a record of frequent absence. He used all his vacation and sick leave days and frequently requested additional leave without pay. His supervisor and co-workers expressed great frustration because his absenteeism caused bottlenecks in paperwork, created low morale in the office, and required others to do his work in addition to their own. On the other hand, he felt he was entitled to take his earned time and additional time off without pay. Was he right?

The Role of Conscience

CHAPTER 6

Is the basis of morality each person's own conscience?

The term *conscience* is usually taken too much for granted. In such cases, familiarity breeds thoughtlessness. Precisely what is conscience? How does it originate? How trustworthy is it as a moral guide? Can it be developed? Too often we overlook these pertinent questions when we think about conscience.

Over the centuries philosophers have disagreed in their definitions of conscience. Some have defined it as the voice of God speaking directly to the individual soul. The problem with this definition is that in cases where conscience does not inform a person that an act is wrong (or misinforms the person), the implication is that God has failed that person. Such an idea is unacceptable to religious people. Others have defined conscience as a mirror of custom, which reflects what our culture has taught us. This definition also creates a problem: It leaves unexplained those cases in which conscience directs us to *defy* custom.

Still others have argued that conscience is a special sense, a moral sense, that is innate in human beings. This may come closest to being a workable definition, but it also poses difficulties that must not be overlooked. The term *sense* usually suggests an essentially developed faculty associated with a particular organ—the sense of sight, with the eyes; the sense of hearing, with the ears; and so on. Conscience cannot be *that kind* of sense. (When we say, "My conscience is bothering me" or "My conscience is clear," we are not talking of any *physical* condition.)

What kind of sense can conscience be? It is the kind that depends upon the nurturing it receives over the years to realize its potential. It is the kind that must be trained to be trustworthy. Although no comparison can be completely accurate, we might compare conscience to

42

our sense of appreciation of beauty. Like conscience, this sense is present in everyone, is not a physical phenomenon, is subject to a variety of influences, and depends for its highest realization on conscious development.

Differences in Development

Simple observation will demonstrate that the intensity of conscience differs from person to person. Even as small children most of us have perceived, however vaguely, that our playmates and relatives appear to differ widely in this phenomenon that we can speak of only obliquely. Preschoolers will often grab toys away from others. Some of them will never show (and if externals are a mirror to internal states of mind, never *feel*) the slightest remorse. Yet others will be so aware of the offensiveness of such behavior that they will immediately be so saddened, so repentant, that their faces will reflect clearly the wretchedness they feel. Hours later they will still be trying to make amends.

The classmates of a grade school stutterer will vary greatly in their attitude toward him. Many will treat him as a nonperson, an object to tease and taunt and mimic. Some will simply know no better and will be unaware that their actions are wrong. Others will at some moment sense that they have caused him pain and will feel ashamed of their behavior.

Such differences in conscience are observable in adults as well. Some people are very sensitive to the effects of their actions, acutely aware when they have done wrong. Others are relatively insensitive, unconscious of their offenses, free from feelings of remorse. They live their lives uninterested in self-examination or self-criticism, seldom even considering whether something *should* be done. Others see right and wrong as applying to only a limited number of matters—sexual behavior, for example, and deportment within the family. The affairs of citizenship and business or professional conduct are, to them, outside the sphere of morality. Still others were at one time morally sensitive, but have succeeded in neutralizing the promptings of conscience with elaborate rationalizations. When Claude's wife expresses disapproval of his cramming the hotel's soap and towels and rugs and bed-spreads into his suitcase, he says, "Look, the hotels in this country expect you to take a few souvenirs. They build the cost into their room rates. If I take a bit more than they've allowed for, they write it off on their tax returns."

Finally, there are the extremists: the scrupulous and the lax. Scrupulous people are morally sensitive beyond reasonableness, often to the point of compulsion. They see moral faults where there are none. Every action, however trivial—whether to peel the potatoes or cook them whole, whether to polish the car today or tomorrow—is an excruciating moral dilemma. Their counterparts at the other pole are virtually without conscience, using other people as things, unmindful of their status as persons, pursuing only what satisfies the almighty *me*.

The Shapers of Conscience

The kind of conscience we have, the scope of its influence on our behavior, and its intensity are shaped by three forces: our own conscious moral direction, natural endowment, and conditioning.

Conscious Moral Direction Conscious moral direction is the self-determined force of conscience, the aspect that is freely chosen independently of other influences. It is this force that we are most aware of. When we behave in a certain way, we are usually quite confident that we have a choice, that we are choosing, and that there is no influence operating on our behavior but what we freely *will*. This is much less often the case, however, than most of us are aware. More often, the two other forces influence the development and action of our conscience significantly.

Natural Endowment A person's basic temperament and level and kind of intelligence are largely "in the genes." That temperament and intelligence play a considerable role in shaping the total personality. The person with a practical intelligence and the person with a philosophic intelligence will not have the same potential for ethical analysis or the same potential for perceptiveness in moral issues. This is not to say that the two kinds of intelligence are mutually exclusive. Some people, happily, have both. There are, after all, philosophers of science and philosophers of technology; and the contributions of mathematicians to modern philosophy have been considerable. Neither is it to say that those with more philosophical potential always use that potential, or that this factor is always so dominant as to make them have more developed consciences. It is to say that the kind of intelligence one has, like the degree of intelligence, opens some doors of potentiality and closes others. Similarly, the basic temperament, largely a matter of one's metabolism, poses certain obstacles and opportunities in the development of conscience.

For example, the vivacious, energetic person, quick of movement and speech, who constantly performs in metabolic overdrive, may tend to be somewhat less disposed to careful analysis of past actions than the slower, more reflective person. The impulsive person, impatient to do and have done, may be virtually incapable of prior reflection. Conscience, in this case, may operate only after the fact. It is not, of course, a matter of one disposition, one metabolic rate being preferable to another. Each presents some fertile areas for the development and use of conscience, and each presents some barren ones.

Conditioning Conditioning is the most neglected shaper of conscience. Yet, ironically, it is in many ways the most important. Conditioning may be defined as the myriad effects of our environment: the people, places, institutions, ideas, and values we are exposed to as we grow and develop. We are conditioned first by our early social and religious training from parents. This influence may be partly conscious and partly unconscious on their part, and indirect as well as direct. It is so pervasive that all our later attitudes—political, economic, sociological, psychological, theological—in some way bear its imprint.

If children are brought up in an ethnocentric environment—that is, one in which the group (race, nationality, culture, or special value system) believes it is superior to others—research shows that they will tend to be less tolerant than other people. More specifically they will tend to make hard right-wrong, good-bad classifications. If they cannot

identify with a group, they must oppose it. In addition, they will tend
to need an "out group," some outsiders whom they can blame for real
and imagined wrongs. This in turn makes it difficult or impossible for
them to identify with humanity as a whole or to achieve undistorted
understanding of others.[1]

In addition, ethnocentric people, even as children, show an inability to deal with complex situations. The result is that the very ways
such people learn to see and think about their daily affairs with other
people and ideas follow the path of oversimplification. Their way of
thinking demands simple solutions to problems, even to problems that
do not admit of simple solutions.[2]

The influence of such training on conscience is obvious. Although
few of us are subjected to a purely ethnocentric environment as children, elements of it are common in most environments in one way or
another. The effects on us, though less dramatic and pronounced, are
nevertheless real and a significant shaping force on our conscience.

We are also conditioned by our encounters with brothers, sisters,
relatives, friends. We see a sister's observance or disregard of family
rules or her habit of lying to parents. An uncle brings a present he has
stolen from work. Our playmates cheat in games. More important, we
see not only these actions, but the reactions of the people themselves
and of others who observe them. We are witness to all the moral con-
tradictions, all the petty hypocrisies of those around us. We act ourselves, now in observance of some parental rule, then against another,
and we sense pleasure or pain. We imitate others' strategies for
justifying questionable behavior.

Next we are conditioned by our experiences in grade school, by
our widening circle of acquaintances, and perhaps by our beginning
contact with institutional religion. We perceive similarities and differences in the attitudes of our teachers and classmates. We observe their
behavior, form impressions, sense (quite subliminally and vaguely, to
be sure) the level and development of their consciences. We meet and
learn from our priest, minister, or rabbi. Perhaps in all these situations
it is not the formal so much as the informal contact, the mere introduction to their personalities, habits, patterns of behavior, that affects

us in dramatic, though subconscious, ways. Memory clouds; experience remains indelible.

We are then conditioned by our contact with people, places, and ideas through books, TV, newspapers, and magazines. Day after day, year after year, the contact expands—from the quiz show and soap opera we watch when we come home from school, to the evening news, to the situation comedy that suggests, on occasion, the response of laughter to situations we were taught to deplore, to the forbidden books and magazines we nervously study in the suspicious quiet of our rooms. Through experiences numerous beyond calculation and varied beyond recall, our views are by turns confused and made clear, our parental teachings challenged and reinforced.

A Balanced View of Conscience

Conscience is important. Indeed, it is the most important single criterion of right and wrong that we have as individuals. As the saying goes, it is the "proximate norm of morality." For this reason, when circumstances demand an immediate moral choice, we should follow our conscience. (The only alternative would be to violate it, to choose to do what our best impulse at that time brands as immoral.) However, whenever circumstances allow us time to reflect on the choice conscience recommends, we should use that time to analyze the issue critically and to consider the possibility that a different choice might be better.

In short, we should follow our conscience, but not blindly. True freedom, true individuality, and real moral growth lie in examining conscience, evaluating its promptings, purging it of bad influences and error, and reinforcing it with searching ethical inquiry and penetrating ethical judgment. The chapters that follow contain helpful criteria for further developing your conscience.

Accordingly, for our purposes in examining moral issues in this and subsequent chapters, the answer "It's a matter for the individual's conscience to decide" will be inappropriate. Let's consider a few cases to see exactly why. A high school girl hears a rumor that a classmate is a shoplifter. Is she morally justified in repeating the story to her best friend if she makes the friend promise not to "tell a soul"? A 13-year-old boy walks into his neighborhood grocery store and asks the grocer for a pack of cigarettes "for my mother." The grocer knows the mother doesn't smoke and that the boy is too young to buy cigarettes legally. Should she sell them to him? A weapons manufacturer has an opportunity to make a big and very profitable sale to the ruler of a small foreign country. He knows the ruler is a tyrant who oppresses his people and governs by terror. Is it right for him to sell the weapons? A college student's friends are all sleeping with their boyfriends and are urging her to "loosen up" and follow their example. (Her boyfriend is not opposed to the idea.) She can't decide, and the more she ponders the matter, the more confused she gets. What should she do?

Whatever we decide is right in these cases, we should go beyond leaving the matter to the individual's conscience. If we say that in the first three cases, we are saying, in effect, "Any action is acceptable," for we can have no way of knowing exactly what those people's consciences will prompt them to do. If we say it in the case of the college student, we are evading the issue, for her dilemma is deciding whether the promptings of her conscience are reasonable.

INQUIRIES

1 For each of the following cases, decide whether the person's conscience was correct. That is, decide whether the action it directed her or him to take (or silently approved) is ethically justifiable. Explain your reasoning.

(a) Broderick stops at a pay phone to make a call. As he is talking, he absentmindedly fingers the coin return and finds a dime someone has carelessly forgotten. When he is finished talking, he pockets the coin and walks away. Halfway down the block, he feels guilty for taking it. He returns to the booth and deposits it in the coin return.

(b) A doctor is driving down the highway late at night. She sees a car in the opposite lane swerve sharply off the road and plunge down an embankment. No other cars are around. Her first impulse as a physician is to stop and assist the victims. However, she remembers that the state has no "Good Samaritan law" to protect her from a malpractice lawsuit. Her conscience tells her she is justified in driving on.

(c) A candidate for the local school board has heard the rumor that her opponent gives "wild parties." As she proceeds with her campaign, she visits the homes of many voters. She makes it a point to tell everyone what she has heard about her opponent, always adding, "Of course, it's only a rumor that no one has yet proven to be true." She believes sincerely that it would be dishonest of her not to inform them about the rumor, so that they can evaluate it before voting.

(d) A professor in graduate school has several student assistants, talented young men and women pursuing doctorates. He regularly uses their research findings in his own scholarly writing, without crediting them either in the text of his articles and books or in the footnotes. "It's part of their job to do research for me," he reasons; "the money they receive from their fellowships for doing the research is credit enough." His conscience does not trouble him.

(e) In order to beat out the competition for a summer gardener's job at a nearby estate, Alan agreed to work for a wage somewhat lower than the standard of the area. The owner and her family are at the estate only on weekends and Alan works alone. Although his workday is fixed—9 to 5, Monday through Friday— he arrives late and leaves early on most days and occasionally takes an afternoon off. He does not feel guilty because his employer is paying him less than others would have worked for.

(f) An enterprising black real estate broker hires a white man and woman to buy a house in a white neighborhood and then transfer title to her. She then visits the white residents of the neighborhood and explains that she owns one house already and plans to buy others and sell them to black families. She tells each white resident that some other white neighbor has secretly agreed to sell. Everyone becomes frightened that property values will plummet and many are tricked into selling to the broker at much lower prices than their homes are worth. The broker then sells the homes to black families for what they are really worth. Not only does she feel morally blameless, but she regards herself as a heroine of sorts, a fighter against discrimination in housing.

(g) Fred is the oldest of seven children of a widow. He is an honor student in a technical program at a nearby junior college. He pays his way by stealing automobile tires, radios, and stereo tape decks and selling them. When he first took up this part-time "occupation," he felt a little guilty. But he no longer does, for he decided that no one is really injured: The owners will be somewhat inconvenienced but not deprived because their insurance will cover replacement costs.

2 The following people all have clear consciences. Decide whether they are entitled to them and explain your decision.

(a) George believes strongly that drug use and dealing are a personal matter, outside the sphere of morality. He sells marijuana, cocaine, heroin, anything. Whatever there is a market for, he will deal in.

(b) Gus specializes in LSD, which he laces liberally with strychnine to increase his profits.

(c) Mary Jane sells marijuana.

(d) Connie believes strongly that the use of any drug is a crutch and that hard drugs ruin lives. She volunteers to be an undercover agent at her college, without pay.

3 The consciences of the people in the following cases are confused. As a result, the people cannot decide whether the actions they are contemplating are morally right. Decide for them and present the rationale for your position.

(a) A married couple discover that their 22-year-old daughter, a college senior, is a lesbian. They are shocked and dismayed, for they regard this as moral degeneracy. They are thinking of refusing to attend her graduation and refusing to welcome her in their home until she renounces this sexual preference.

(b) A student is taking a composition course in college. Her assignment is to write on the morality of war. Back in her room she moans aloud that she doesn't know where to begin with such a complex subject. One of her roommates declares where she stands on the issue. The other challenges her view. In time, several students wander into the room and get involved in the ensuing discussion. One goes out and gets a term paper she did on a similar subject. She reads it aloud and is interrupted from time to time as someone disputes a statement or expands upon it. After an hour or so, the session breaks up, leaving the student who didn't know where to begin with a different problem: deciding to what extent, if any, she is justified in using in her paper the facts and opinions she heard from the others.

(c) Harry has been an officer in the police department of his small city for a year. He has seen many violations of department policy: squad car teams pulling over on lonely streets and sleeping during evening shifts, officers receiving "quiet money" from gamblers and dope pushers, officers conducting sexual commerce with women in the station house while on duty, sergeants and lieutenants spending whole shifts at home and altering duty records to cover their absences. Harry is seriously considering turning these men in, but he is confused about where his loyalty should lie.

(d) An airline pilot goes for his regular medical checkup. The doctor discovers that he has developed a heart murmur. The pilot has only a month to go before he is eligible for retirement. The doctor knows this, and wonders whether, under these unusual circumstances, she is justified in withholding the information about the pilot's condition.

4 Animal lovers in a suburb of Los Angeles picketed a parochial school to protest the action of a priest-educator. The priest had drowned ten cats because they were too noisy and messy. He explained that his action had been "humane" and added, "I buried them. They're fertilizing our rose bushes."[3] Apparently, the priest's conscience didn't bother him. Should it have?

5   It is common practice for workers in the electronics industry to change employers frequently. Karen advanced from technician to product design engineer for Kludge Demiconductor. Widgit Ware hired her away at a considerable advance in salary. She shared all of the product design knowledge she had gained at Kludge with her new employer, thus aiding Widgit to gain a competitive edge in the market. Karen felt perfectly justified because she was personally responsible for much of the product design at her old firm, and she felt that Widgit paid her well for her knowledge.

6   A cosmetologist in a local beauty salon enjoys a high sales record and popularity with his clients. He believes that being attractive is extremely important and that his job is to help his clients feel that they are or could be attractive. Although he realizes that some of his compliments are false and that some of the products he sells do not live up to advertising claims, he feels he is performing a public service by making people feel good about themselves.

A STRATEGY

The Basic Criteria

CHAPTER 7

If the majority isn't necessarily right, feelings can be capricious, and conscience is imperfect, how can the moral quality of an action be determined?

A t this point in our search for a basis for evaluating moral issues, we may feel a sense of frustration and even of futility. If our ethical stance was anchored to one of the standards we have found insufficient, we may feel particularly adrift and insecure. We may even be led to conclude that no basis is available.

But let's reflect on what we've discarded. Are the positions "The majority must be right," "Trust your feelings," and "Follow your conscience" trustworthy guides to independent judgment? No. They lead to unwitting, uncritical dependence on others' views, or on our conditioning, which amounts to much the same thing. The conclusions such positions lead us to in moral issues are not judgments; they are easy substitutes for judgment. Although they have value in their place, when taken out of their place and made to substitute for judgment, they are no more than conditioned reflexes, like the droolings of Pavlov's dog.

To develop a sound and meaningful basis for discussing moral issues, we must find a standard for judging the morality of actions, a standard that is acceptable to men and women of various moral perspectives. In other words, we must find a standard that reflects the principles that most ethical systems have in common. By proceeding from the considerations that are fundamental to all, or at least most, ethical systems, we can set aside our normal defensiveness about our own positions, free ourselves from the entanglements of prefabricated interpretations, and elevate our dialogue to a more analytic and objective level.

The Underlying Principle: Respect for Persons

At least one important principle underlies almost all ethical systems.* It is the principle of *respect for persons*. This principle includes three requirements, which Errol E. Harris explains as follows:

> First, that each and every person should be regarded as worthy of sympathetic consideration, and should be so treated; secondly, that no person should be regarded by another as a mere possession, or used as a mere instrument, or treated as a mere obstacle, to another's satisfaction; and thirdly, that persons are not and ought never to be treated in any undertaking as mere expendables.[1]

When we say that this principle underlies most ethical systems, we are not saying that it is always interpreted in the same way, or that it is always observed, or that it is always given precedence over other principles. We have already noted that some primitive cultures interpret "person" to mean "member of my tribe," and feel justified in treating aliens as nonpersons. (The practice of slavery in American history is based on a similar kind of interpretation.) Likewise, people may endorse the principle of respect for persons, but have lapses in its observance, or may at times subordinate it to other values, such as the good of society as a whole. One such lapse that is frequently ignored occurs when people get so concerned with serving others that they forget that

---

*An exception is the aberrant system of the Dobuans, which we noted in Chapter 2.

they themselves are persons and therefore are worthy of the same consideration they give others in their moral evaluations.

Saying that the principle of respect for persons underlies most ethical systems means, rather, that it is either stated or implied in most systems and that it can be found operating in the moral reasoning of those systems.

Three Basic Criteria

Three basic criteria for judging moral issues proceed from the principle of respect for persons and are used in the moral reasoning of most ethical systems. These criteria are *obligations, ideals,* and *consequences.* Emphasis on them differs from system to system, and the theoretical formulations of ethicists may focus on one to the virtual exclusion of the others. Nevertheless, they are found to inform the reasoning of most ethicists about particular moral issues. For this reason they will be our principal concern in this chapter and subsequent chapters.

Obligations Every significant human action occurs, directly or indirectly, in a context of relationships with others. And relationships usually imply *obligations;* that is, restrictions on our behavior, demands to do something or avoid doing it. The most obvious kind of obligation is a formal agreement. Whenever a person enters into a contract with someone—for example, to sell something or to perform a service—we consider that person ethically (as well as legally) bound to live up to his or her agreement.

There are other kinds of obligations, too. There are obligations of friendship that demand, for example, the keeping of confidences. There are obligations of citizenship that in a democracy demand concern for the conduct of government and responsible participation in the electoral process. There are business obligations. The employer or supervisor, for example, is morally bound to use fair hiring practices, judge workers impartially, and pay them a reasonable wage that is consistent with the demands of their position and the quality of their work. The employee, in turn, is morally bound to do a job as efficiently

55

and competently as he or she is able to. Both have moral obligations to their customers.

In addition, there are professional obligations. Lawyers are obligated to protect the interests of their clients, doctors to promote or restore the health of their patients, teachers to advance the knowledge and wisdom of their students, elected officials to serve the interests of their constituents.

When we say obligations bind morally, we mean they exist to be honored. To honor them is right; to dishonor them is wrong. The fact that what is considered an obligation may be found to be illegitimate does not refute this idea. An illegitimate obligation is a contradiction in terms: If it is illegitimate, then it is not an obligation. Even if the action we are required or forbidden to perform is morally insignificant, the obligation has moral force. Thus, if Edna promises not to go to the carnival without notifying Carl in advance, to break the promise without compelling reason is to do wrong. Surely there is nothing wrong in going to the carnival or in not calling Carl beforehand. It is the *promise* that binds Edna.[2]

Ideals In the general sense *ideals* are notions of excellence, goals that bring greater harmony in one's self and between self and others. In ethics ideals are also specific concepts that assist us in applying the principle of respect for persons in our moral judgments. Some common ideals that figure prominently in ethical reasoning are fairness, tolerance, compassion, loyalty, forgiveness, amity, and peace.

Different cultures interpret the same ideal differently, of course. As we have seen, the way a culture interprets its ideals and relates one to another will affect its judgment of particular actions. The Eskimo accepts the ideal of respect for the aged, but some of the Eskimo's ways of honoring it—for instance, walling them up in an igloo to die when they are too old to contribute to the community and are a drain on its resources—are somewhat different from ours. Furthermore, the same ideal of justice that we honor may impel someone in some culture to do something we would never think of doing: for instance, to cut out the tongue of one who has uttered a taboo word. These variations in the ways of viewing and pursuing ideals surely pose exquisite dilemmas for those engaged in cross-cultural studies and those whose occupations involve them directly with other cultures (diplomats, for example, and medical and religious missionaries). They present less difficulty for us in the examination of our own culture.

Consequences *Consequences* are what happen as a result of an action, the beneficial or harmful effects that flow from the action and affect the people involved, including, of course, the person performing the action. Some consequences are physical; others are emotional. Some occur immediately; others occur only with the passing of time. Some are intended by the person performing the act; others are unintended. Finally, some consequences may be obvious, and others may be very subtle and hidden by appearances. The ethicist is concerned with all significant consequences of actions in a moral context. Because consequences can be complex and difficult to pinpoint, ethical analysis very often requires not merely an examination of indisputable facts, but speculation about possibilities and probabilities.

Analyzing Issues

As your analyses of the inquiries in the first six chapters of this book have undoubtedly revealed, the job of examining issues and making judgments can be a difficult one, even when the cases are relatively simple. The fact that you now have a set of criteria to use can be of considerable help to you if you apply the criteria thoughtfully and systematically. The following approach will help you accomplish this:

Step One Study the details of the case carefully. Look closely at any circumstances that set it apart from otherwise similar cases. Keep in mind that "circumstances alter cases." Suppose, for example, that a computer operator used her employer's computer for her own personal project. Is such an action morally acceptable? It is impossible to give a meaningful answer without knowing more of the details of the case. You must identify the important questions that a meaningful answer would depend upon. *Did she use the computer on her own time or on* *company time? Was she expressly forbidden to use it? Was her personal project in any way competitive with or harmful to her employer's business?* These are the key questions.

If, as often happens, you have insufficient details about a case to answer one or more of your important questions, speculate about *possible* answers. For example, if the issue were the firing of a teacher because of his homosexuality and you didn't know the specific cause of his being fired, you would consider the possibilities that (a) he was propagandizing for homosexuality in his class, (b) he was enticing his own students, and (c) he was merely living with another homosexual. (For the first two causes the firing may be morally defensible, but for the third it would undoubtedly be indefensible.)

Step Two Identify specific criteria that are relevant to the case. In other words, ask these questions: Are there any *obligations?* What *ideals* are involved? What are the *consequences* of the case? Whom will they affect? In what way? After identifying the criteria, decide where the emphasis should lie. Sometimes the issue will be mainly a matter of obligation; at other times an ideal will be most important; at still other times the consequences will be most important. Not infrequently, the force of all three will be very nearly equal.

Step Three Determine all possible choices of action that are (or, in the case of a past action, were) available. This consideration can have a significant bearing on the judgment of an action. Occasionally an action that would normally be considered immoral will be justifiable because no reasonable alternative course of action is available. For example, although the deliberate killing of an individual is wrong, a police officer is justified in shooting a berserk man who has taken a woman hostage and suddenly begins choking and stabbing her. More commonly, one or more alternative choices will be open to a person. By determining what they are, you increase your chances of making a reasonable moral judgment.

Step Four In light of your findings in steps one through three, decide which action is most ethical.

This four-step approach will help you cut through the confusion that surrounds many complex moral issues, overcome indecision, and reach a judgment, and it will also help you express that judgment to others. Let's look at two cases and see how the approach works in practice.

The Case of Agatha's Relationship

> Agatha, a married woman with three children, is in the habit of seeing her unmarried minister alone rather often. Since the relationship began several years ago in a mutual interest in intellectual and social issues, it has grown and expanded. Agatha's daily visits to the minister's home and his frequent visits to hers, sometimes when her husband is at home, but often when he is not, have become the subject of community gossip and are threatening both their reputations. There has been no overt sexual dimension to the relationship; it has remained platonic. Lately, however, Agatha has begun to have sexual thoughts about the minister. Is it morally wrong for her to continue the relationship?

Analysis Step One   You would note the details given and identify the following important questions, which are not answered in the statement of the case:

How old are the children?

How solid and mutually nourishing was Agatha's relationship with her husband before she began her relationship with the minister?

If there have been problems in her relationship with her husband, have they discussed them? Have they made any progress in solving them?

Has Agatha discussed with the minister the direction in which their relationship seems to be heading? If so, what was his reaction?

What other possibilities does Agatha have for social life and intellectual fulfillment?

Analysis Step Two   You would identify the obligations, ideals, and consequences involved in the case. There are several *obligations*. Agatha has an obligation to herself to exercise her intellect and realize her potential. As a wife she has an obligation to her husband (as he does to her) to build and nurture a mutually satisfying physical and emotional relationship. As a mother she has an obligation to provide a home and atmosphere conducive to her children's physical, emotional, moral, and intellectual development. The minister, too, has at least one relevant obligation—to serve his congregation's religious and spiritual needs.

At least two *ideals* are involved: marital fidelity and honesty with self and friends. (We might also note the traditional but now frequently questioned ideal of the minister as a model of scandal-free behavior.) Marital fidelity has, of course, more dimensions than the sexual: A spouse can be faithful in body but not in mind, in attitude, in heart. The ideal of honesty with self demands that Agatha not deceive herself about the probable direction of her relationship with the minister.

What about the *consequences* of continuing the relationship? It is unlikely that Agatha's marriage will be strengthened by continuing it. In fact, the reverse is a distinct possibility. Her sexual thoughts could easily lead to sexual involvement, which would break her bond of faith with her husband and threaten her marriage. At the very least it would undoubtedly create (or increase) tension in her relationship with him. Even if that tension were never directly expressed and Agatha and her husband worked hard to be loving parents, the fact that the tension existed would affect the children indirectly.

Neither is the effect of the relationship on the minister's vocation likely to be beneficial. It could destroy his effectiveness as a minister and jeopardize his position, particularly if he belongs to a conservative religious denomination.

Analysis Step Three You would consider the possible actions open to Agatha and decide that she does not have to allow events to take whatever course they will. She has several alternatives. She could break off with the minister, explaining to him that she is doing so to save her marriage. Or she could see him less frequently and never alone or in his or her home. (This would be more effective if it were combined with an attempt to renew her relationship with her husband

and find other social and intellectual outlets.) On the other hand, she could obtain a legal separation from her husband.

Analysis Step Four   In light of your analysis you would probably conclude that the three criteria—obligations, ideals, and consequences — are of nearly equal force and all of them suggest that it is wrong for Agatha to continue the relationship with the minister, at least in its present form, and that despite the satisfaction she and the minister get from it and despite the fact that it is not tainted with sexual infidelity, it does cause harm and will very likely cause additional harm in the future. In terms of which course of action is the most supportable on ethical grounds, you would probably reason as follows:

If Agatha's relationship with her husband was reasonably healthy before she met the minister, she should end the relationship with the minister or at least severely curtail it. If her relationship with her husband had already deteriorated and is beyond rebuilding, then she should leave him. The age of her children should be a factor in the decision of whether to leave her husband. If she does leave, the possible effects of the scandal on the minister should influence her decision of whether to continue her relationship with him after leaving.

The Case of Dumbrowski's House

Mr. Barker is returning to a town he once lived in and a position he once held. He and his wife visit several real estate brokers there in hopes of finding a house. One broker mentions that Mr. Dumbrowski's house will soon be for sale. "Oh," Barker says, "I know Dumbrowski; is he leaving the area?" The broker explains that he is not, but is moving to a larger house she showed him because his family has outgrown their present home. As they are driving to inspect the Dumbrowski property, Barker casually asks the broker which house Dumbrowski is buying. The broker tells him. She innocently adds that he is paying $78,000 for it.

After leaving the broker, Barker goes directly to the owner of the house Dumbrowski is planning to buy, inspects it, is impressed with what he sees, and says to the owner, "Look, I

61

know Dumbrowski has offered you $78,000. I'll pay $79,000, and what's more, you won't have to pay any broker's commission." The owner agrees and Barker buys the house. Was Barker's behavior unethical?

Analysis Step One   After a close reading of this case, you would probably decide that, unlike the case of Agatha's relationship, the statement of this case leaves no significant questions unanswered.

Analysis Step Two   Whether Barker violated a *legal* obligation between the broker and the owner of the house is a question that does not concern us here. But did he violate a *moral obligation?* Clearly, the broker did not give him the information so that he could use it against her interests. She trusted him and he used the information in a way that injured her financially. The issue comes down to whether we are *obligated* not to act on information someone carelessly gives us. It may be tempting to say yes, but it is not reasonable. Whatever we wish Barker had done, or conclude he should have done, we cannot make the case on the basis of obligation.

What *ideals* are involved? The obvious one is fairness. The action most in keeping with this ideal would be for Barker to have refused to take advantage of his knowledge about the house, to have considered it sold to Dumbrowski and not interfere. At very least, if he felt impelled to outbid Dumbrowski, he could have approached the owner in such a way that the broker's commission would be paid. After all, without her help, however inadvertently it was given, he would not have known about the property.

The *consequences* (on others) of Barker's action are plain enough. The broker lost the commission. Dumbrowski and his family lost the house they almost bought.

Analysis Step Three   Unless the house Dumbrowski was planning to buy was the only available house in town, Barker did have an alternative to outbidding Dumbrowski. He could have asked the broker that mentioned the house to him and his wife, or some other broker, to show them other houses.

62

Analysis Step Four   In light of your analysis you would undoubtedly conclude that the three criteria—obligations, ideals, and consequences —are not of equal force. There is no real obligation involved. The consequences, though unfortunate, are not in themselves sufficiently harmful to make the action wrong. Yet Barker's action is morally wrong because it is a gross violation of the ideal of fairness.

In each of the above cases, and in all the cases you encounter, the moral action is the action that most fully honors the obligations, ideals, and consequences involved, the action that best *fits the situation*. It is the action that *ought* to be chosen not just by the person in the case in question, but by *anyone in the same circumstances*. As subsequent chapters will reveal, the solutions to moral problems are seldom perfect solutions; they are only the best choices from among the imperfect solutions that are available.

A Caution About Generalizing

The temptation to move beyond the criteria we have been discussing and to develop a set of firm generalizations or "rules" of ethics is a common temptation. Although it arises from a very legitimate desire to simplify and streamline the process of analysis, it usually causes many more problems than it solves and is best avoided.*

Let's say we are analyzing a situation in which someone has taken something belonging to someone else. If we begin by applying an unqualified general rule, such as "It is wrong to take what does not belong to us," *we will have already judged the situation in question.* After making such a judgment, any analysis we do is likely to be little more than a listing of the reasons to support our predetermined conclusion. Like the juror who makes up his mind that the defendant is guilty the moment he sees him, we may appear to be weighing the evidence and

---

*It is possible to construct ethical rules that are so carefully shaped and qualified as to withstand even the most subtle objections. But that kind of construction is an activity that only the most advanced students of ethics should undertake. The safest and most profitable focus is on individual cases, not on generalizations.

may even believe that we are. Yet, in fact, we will have already made up our minds.

But, someone might object, what is wrong with starting with a rule like "It's wrong to take something that does not belong to us"? Doesn't such a generalization fit most cases? Certainly, and that is just the problem. The generalization about the wrongness of taking what doesn't belong to us would cover numerous situations from bank robbery to embezzlement to stealing hubcaps and even to pocketing the extra change the supermarket cashier gave us by mistake. But it doesn't cover the exceptions, such as finding some change in a public telephone booth or taking in a stray dog and (after advertising in the local paper and not finding the owner) keeping it. In judging any particular case we must be concerned with precisely that: whether there is anything about the case that makes it the exception to the rule.

It is tempting to protest that there must be some generalization that applies in all cases. "Do unto others as you would have them do unto you," comes to mind. What, after all, is more basic to morality than this Golden Rule found in virtually all advanced moral systems? And yet, as Paul A. Freund has pointed out, even this rule has its exception, for a masochist's application of it would prompt him to torture others.[3]

An interesting illustration of the danger of relying on sweeping ethical generalizations and the importance of inquiring into the circumstances of the case occurred some years ago. In Willowbrook State Hospital, an institution for the retarded, medical doctors intentionally infected entering children with infectious hepatitis virus. On first consideration, such behavior seems outrageous. It calls to mind the barbarisms of Nazi concentration camps. In fact, not a few critics regarded the action as precisely such a moral atrocity.

The details of the situation, however, undermine that hasty judgment. It was known that a mild form of hepatitis was rife in the institution. Historical data showed that most of the newly admitted children would be infected by natural means. By deliberately infecting newly admitted patients, the doctors could assure them a milder case of the disease, and they could be given special housing and care while ill. Moreover, the plan had been reviewed and approved by several agencies, and parental consent was obtained before a child was infected.[4]

The tendency to respond to issues with unqualified generalizations, though natural enough, should not be indulged. The people we are writing for or speaking with deserve better from us. Every important ethical issue demands our careful attention, not only to its similarity to other issues, but also to its dissimilarity, to its uniqueness. To give less, to merely mouth an overall, ready-made response is not to use moral rules, but to be used by them; not to be guided by our experience, but to be controlled by it. It takes wisdom to know when the case at hand fits the rule and when it is the exception to it. Such wisdom does not come easily. And if we substitute generalization for analysis, it does not come at all.

INQUIRIES

Use the approach explained in the chapter to analyze each of the cases that follow.

1 A seventh-grade teacher divides his class into teams to research some history topics and report to the class. Each team consists of four students. One team presents a report that is excellent in substance. However, two members of the team behave childishly while making their contributions, so the overall presentation is flawed. The teacher lowers the team's mark a full letter grade. Since the grade recorded for each team member is identical to the team grade, each member is penalized.

2 A businessman is waiting for an elevator in his office building. A stranger motions him aside and whispers, "Wanna buy a fur coat for your wife? Two hundred dollars. No questions asked. What say?" He opens a large paper bag to reveal the coat. The businessman looks at it, touches it, and realizes that the coat is unquestionably mink and worth at least ten times what the man is asking for it. He takes out his wallet, hands over the $200, and takes the bag.

3   A common method for dispatching animals in slaughterhouses is to hit them on the head with a sledgehammer as many times as necessary to drive them into semiconsciousness, then to impale one of their rear legs, hoist them into the air, and slit their throats, leaving them to bleed to death.

4   A woman learns that her son-in-law fathered an illegitimate child several years before he met her daughter. (He and his wife have been happily married for ten years. They are childless.) She is sure her daughter is not aware of this and has reason to doubt that she would ever find out about it by herself. The woman feels obliged to tell her, however, and does so.

5   The executives of a large company are planning their advertising campaign for the coming year. They would prefer to use a simple and honest approach, but they know that their competitors use devious psychological approaches and even outright lies in their advertising. The executives fear that if they do not use the same approaches as their competitors, their company's profits will suffer and they may lose their jobs. They decide to play it safe and use those approaches.

6   A man and woman, both college students, have been living together off campus for three years. They have never considered marrying, and it has always been implicit in their relationship that each should be free to leave the other any time he or she wishes. Unexpectedly, the woman becomes pregnant. Since she is opposed to abortion, she resigns herself to having the child. When she is seven months pregnant, the man decides to leave her. One day when she is out shopping for groceries, he gathers his belongings, scribbles a hasty note ("Our relationship was beautiful while it lasted, but it's over.") and leaves.

7   The scene is a large room at a political convention. The members of a state delegation are entering to caucus about an important issue.

The meeting is closed to the public and press. However, one enterprising reporter has anticipated the caucus and is carrying forged credentials identifying her as a member of the delegation. Hoping for a news scoop, she flashes her false credentials at the door, moves inside the room, flips on a concealed tape recorder, and mingles with the crowd.

8   A businessman wishes to invest some money in wooded land. He knows that he can sell the trees for lumber, plant more trees, and sell them when they mature. He will be serving the cause of ecology at the same time he makes a modest income. After finding a parcel of land that is appropriate for his purposes, he asks the owner the selling price. The price is so ridiculously low that the man realizes the owner is unaware of the value of the trees as lumber. He ponders whether it is immoral to buy the land at such a price. He decides it is not and buys it.

9   A young woman has a serious kidney disease. She undergoes expensive care while awaiting the availability of a donor's kidney. One day she receives word that a donor has been found. She looks forward happily to the transplant operation. Then she finds out that the donor is an institutionalized mental defective who is unable to understand the nature of the operation and the remote possible danger to him should his other kidney ever become damaged. The surgeon will be removing the organ without his permission. The young woman accepts the kidney anyway.

10   Knowing that after negotiations with management are completed they will get less than they ask for in wages and fringe benefits, some labor unions begin negotiations by demanding more than is reasonable.

11   Allegedly, the U.S. Army is researching mechanical ways to control human behavior. For example, they are conducting experiments with devices that use "flickering light of varying intensity" to render the brain incapable of controlling the body, and devices that emit inaudible sound to confuse the mind and cause pain. (An army spokesman stated that such devices might be useful in controlling crowds.)[5]

12   A newspaper carrier begins his job with enthusiasm. His supervisor explains that once or twice a week, advertising inserts will be delivered with the papers and must be placed inside them. The job of inserting is a time-consuming chore, the supervisor explains, and paper carriers are easily tempted to discard the inserts. However, the supervisor warns, discarding them is grounds for dismissal, because the advertisers pay for them and have a right to expect them to reach the customers. Not only is each newspaper carrier expected to handle his or her own inserts properly, the carrier is also expected to report any other paper carrier who does not do so. Two weeks later, the boy notices that all the other delivery people in his town regularly throw the inserts in a trash barrel. He reports them to his supervisor.

13   Midwestern University is a national football power. The alumni association, which exerts considerable influence on the university's affairs, does not tolerate losing teams or any faculty member or administrator who stands in the way of victory. This year Professor Woebegone has had the misfortune of having Roger Rapid, star halfback, in his mathematics class. Roger is mathematically illiterate. After spending many extra hours with Roger in hopes of dragging him through the course sucessfully, Professor Woebegone has been forced to admit failure. On the final exam Roger has scored 27. Judged by the grading scale in the course, his final average is an F. Since he is a borderline student in other courses, an F will place him on academic probation and he will be ineligible for the last crucial game of the season. Without him the team will surely lose the conference title. Professor Woebegone, who is untenured, may well lose his job. The professor turns in a D+ grade for Roger.

14   A businesswoman realizes that with the local college enrollment burgeoning, an investment in a trailer court will be profitable. It happens, too, that a perfect site is available. The one complication is that the owner of the land, who lives across the highway, would not sell it if he knew it would be put to such use. The businesswoman therefore pays a young married couple to buy it for her. They approach the owner, explain that they want the land to build a home on, and even show him fake building plans. After he sells the land to them, they turn it over to the businesswoman.

15 Residents of a poor neighborhood are plagued with a drug problem. Five pushers operate openly on their streets and brazenly try to entice their children to take "free samples." A committee of residents has approached the police and begged them to arrest the pushers, but they have done nothing. There is reason to believe some of the police are sharing in the proceeds of the drug trade. The residents decide that their only hope for a safe and decent neighborhood for their children is to take the law into their own hands. Accordingly, one calm summer night they unceremoniously execute the five pushers.

16 A nurse in a nursing home dispenses medication to elderly patients. The home is understaffed and, though the existing staff is efficent, there is such a demand on their time that they have difficulty in doing a quality job. The nursing supervisor frequently orders the nurse to give the patients unprescribed tranquilizers to keep them quiet and docile. This allows the staff to attend to critical needs.

17 A large grocery chain orders its personnel department to screen out all grocery clerk applicants who have a prison record, a history of alcohol/drug abuse or mental illness, or are obese.

Considering Obligations

CHAPTER 8

*What do we do in situations where there is more
than a single obligation? How can we reconcile
conflicting obligations?*

In the preceding chapter we noted a number of obligations. All
of them were of the same type: They are known as obligations of
fidelity and represent some formal bond of faith to people or institutions.
This is not, however, the only type of obligation. British ethicist W. D.
Ross has suggested the following four additional types[1]:

Obligations of Reparation. These obligations require us to make
amends for the wrongs we commit by removing, to whatever extent
we can, the harmful consequences caused by those wrongs.

Obligations of Gratitude. These obligations require us to demonstrate
our appreciation for the considerateness others show us. When we
express gratitude in words or deeds, we are not merely extending a
courtesy to others, but are fulfilling a debt their kindness has created
for us.

Obligations of Justice. Obligations of justice demand that we give each
person equal consideration. This does not mean that everyone must
be treated exactly alike; it means that everyone must be given his or
her due and that no partiality be shown to anyone's interests (including our own). Accordingly, differences in treatment should be
in proportion to differences in what the facts show each person
deserves.

Obligations of Beneficence. These obligations require us to do good acts
for their own sake; that is, for no other reason than that they are
good. (Viewing beneficence as an obligation rather than as an ideal
may seem, at first thought, extreme. Yet it is really a logical exten-
sion of an idea central to all ethical systems—that morality consists
not only in avoiding evil, but in doing good.)

When Obligations Conflict

Any one of these obligations may be present by itself in a moral situation. But more often two or more are present; and many times they conflict. In such cases the problem is to choose wisely among them.

The executives of a corporation, for example, must make a difficult decision. Their profit picture has been dismal. If they do not find some way to cut back their expenses, they may be driven into bankruptcy. Since their biggest expense is salaries, it is clear they must make economies there. After analyzing the various operations of the corporation, they determine that they can effect significant economies by curtailing certain services to customers and combining the work of three departments.

This reorganization will make it possible to reduce the work staff by twelve people and result in savings of tens of thousands of dollars. However, each of the people involved has been employed by the company for more than fifteen years, and all are between ages 45 and 55. They are too young for retirement and too old to find other positions very easily.

The dilemma the executives face is the conflict between their obligation to long-time and faithful employees and their obligation to stockholders. Both obligations demand fulfillment. Both obviously cannot be fulfilled. There may be some middle ground possible—some special waiving of the retirement rules that will permit at least some employees to retire early. But even in cases where the executives have the power to grant such a waiver, it is unlikely that they could do it for all twelve people. Choice is unavoidable. They must give preference to one obligation or the other.

Another very common example of a moral dilemma caused by conflicting obligations is that faced by the person who is asked to give a job reference for a colleague or subordinate whom he or she believes may not be able to perform the job in question. The chairman of an academic department, for instance, may be called by his counterpart in another school. "I'm calling about an applicant of ours who worked for you until last year," the caller says. "His name is Dr. Elmo Ryan, and he's applying for a position in sociology." The chairman winces. He

71

remembers Ryan all too well. For three years the poor man struggled to teach his courses well. The chairman visited his classes and tried to help him improve. Several of his colleagues in the department did likewise. Finally, everyone was driven to the same conclusion that the students who were unfortunate enough to be in his classes had long since reached: Ryan simply was not meant to be a teacher.

Now the chairman must answer a direct question about him to a prospective employer. If he tells her the truth about Ryan—that he is a hard-working, personable, cooperative *incompetent*—Ryan will surely lose the job. The chairman feels a certain obligation to Ryan. And yet he feels obligated to the woman on the phone and to all the students Ryan might be assigned to teach. Whatever the chairman decides to do, the decision will not be easy. It will require breaking one obligation.

Does everyone have an obligation to assist in the rehabilitation of former thieves and rapists by giving them a chance to return to society without discrimination? Most of us would agree that there is such an obligation, at least one of beneficence. But if a banker wants to honor that obligation and hire the reformed thief, he or she must also consider the obligation to his or her customers and to the Federal Deposit Insurance Corporation to maintain the security of the bank. If the owners of a girls' camp wish to honor that obligation and hire the reformed rapist, they must consider their obligation to ensure the safety of their clientele.

Weighing the Obligations

In cases where two or more obligations are in conflict for our attention, the best we can do is to *consider the relative importance of each and give preference to the more important one.* (Of course, which obligation is more important is often a decision about which honest, intelligent people may disagree.) To judge well we need a sense of proportion. That is, we need to perceive what balance among the obligations will serve each one to the extent appropriate and thereby make the best of a difficult situation. Whenever both obligations can be partly served, they should be. Whenever only one can be served, the more important one should be.

If a person owes $200 to someone who needs the money, and then, just when he is able to pay, he reads in the paper that contributions are being sought for flood relief in a neighboring state, he may be torn between settling his debt and donating to the flood victims. Which should he do? A rationale could be developed to support either. But a better case could be made for settling his debt, not only because it existed prior to the other, but also because the creditor is in need. The obligation of justice in this case would be more important than the obligation of beneficence. (It is not necessarily so in every case where two obligations conflict. If the creditor did not need the money immediately and the act of charity were to a family that had no income and neither qualified for public assistance nor was likely to find any other private benefactor, beneficence would be more important.)

A merchandiser for a clothing concern is in her busiest season of the year. Moreover, the demands of her job this year are even greater than usual because two very different and daring fashion trends are competing with a well-entrenched mode. The right judgment on the merchandiser's part in assessing the buying public's taste will make a great deal of money for her company; the wrong judgment could ruin the company. Meanwhile her husband, whom she loves, is in a state of depression. He feels he has disappointed her by losing his job, he suspects her (wrongly) of infidelity, and he is given to periods of depression in which he contemplates suicide. The psychiatrist he has been visiting says he is not dangerously ill, but could easily become so. He advises the merchandiser to take her husband on a month's vacation.

What should the wife do? She owes her employer her expert judgment during the next month. Yet she owes her husband help and attention. Which obligation is greater? Most ethicists would undoubtedly rule in favor of the husband for two reasons: first, because the wife's obligation to him probably derives from a solemn vow to care for him ("in sickness and in health"); second, because his condition may be nearing a matter of life and death.

To the extent possible she should, of course, try to serve both obligations. She might, in other words, postpone the vacation for a week or ten days and during that period work a sixteen- or eighteen-hour day. She might even take work with her on the vacation or telephone the office every day to provide whatever guidance she could to her employer. Nevertheless, it would be a graver fault to neglect her husband's needs than to neglect her employer's.

Two Moral Dilemmas

Such choices challenge lawyers and doctors virtually every day. Clarence Darrow, the famous attorney, is said to have won a case by stealing the jury's attention during the prosecutor's summation. He smoked a cigar in which he had placed a wire to prevent the ashes from falling. With each puff the ashes would grow longer . . . and the jury would sit a little farther forward on their chairs. When would those ashes fall? They never did. However brilliant the prosecutor's closing words were, they were ineffective. The jury was too busy watching that cigar to pay any attention to them.

Darrow's bit of vaudeville represented a choice between his obligation to his client and his obligation to courtroom procedure. Obviously, in his judgment no trick was too cheap to play if it helped his client. Was his action morally blameless? Hardly. It was an open and shut case of wrongdoing, though one that we would probably be inclined to approve if our life were in the balance.

A similar case of a lawyer forced to choose between obligations occurred more recently in New York City. Martin Erdmann, a Legal Aid defender, remarked publicly that judgeships today must either be bought or won through political influence. He was brought before the New York City Bar Association for violating the group's code of ethics. (The association recommended that no action be taken against him.) Erdmann had an obligation to the legal profession to protect it from scandal, and he had an obligation to that profession, and to the citizens it represents, to speak out against abuses within the profession. Undoubtedly he judged the latter obligation to be more important.

How do we judge his action? To judge fairly we would have to know more than the details given here or available in the news accounts of his case. If the situation concerning the selection of judges is as he described it, then it makes a mockery of our system of jurisprudence and of the very concept of justice. It cries out for denunciation. His obligation to speak out would indeed take precedence over his obligation to protect his profession. On the other hand, if the situation is not as he described it, or if he wasn't sure and didn't bother to determine the validity of the description, then the obligation to be silent and not scandalize the courts would take precedence. If he had knowledge of some abuses but did not know how widespread they were, the requirement of proportion would have demanded that he modify his statement to reflect his degree of knowledge rather than speak in general terms and indict, by implication, all judges.

The Alabama Syphilis Case

In the summer of 1972 a shocking disclosure was made about a government-sponsored medical experiment that had gone on, unnoticed, for *forty years*. The experiment concerned the effects of syphilis. The Public Health Service began the experiment in Alabama. Its purpose was to determine the extent of the damage that syphilis will do if left untreated. (Its effects, most of them known or at least surmised at the time the experiment was begun, are blindness; deafness; degeneration of the heart, bones, and central nervous system; insanity; and death.) Six hundred black men were selected for the experiment. They were promised free transportation to the hospital, free medical treatment for diseases other than syphilis, and free burial. Apparently they did not receive clear explanations of the possible harm the disease could cause them if left untreated.

Of the six hundred, a third never developed syphilis. Half of those who did received the arsenic-mercury treatment that was standard before the discovery of penicillin. The remaining two hundred got no medication. Even after the discovery of penicillin a decade later and its widespread use as a cure for syphilis, they received no treatment. They remained human guinea pigs.

There were several obligations the researchers should have weighed. First, there was their obligation as physicians to care for their patients. Second, there was their obligation to justice, of respecting other human beings and treating them in a manner consistent with their humanity. Finally, there was their obligation as researchers to serve mankind by seeking cures for deadly diseases. The researchers seem to have ignored the first two obligations completely. Apparently they thought of the men not as patients, but as the "subjects" of the experiment—as phenomena to be studied rather than as persons to be cured. If they recognized the inhumanity of their handling of the two hundred men, they failed to act upon their recognition. (There is a bitter irony in this case. During the very period in which the experiment was conducted, Nazi doctors performed similar barbarities on the inmates of concentration camps. After World War II, at the Nuremberg trials the United States and its allies condemned those doctors for "crimes against humanity.")

The shock felt by every sensitive person at this disclosure reveals the importance of choosing well among conflicting moral obligations. It was not wrong for the doctors in the Alabama case to honor their obligation as researchers. What was wrong was their ignoring the two other obligations, both of which were more important.

Thoroughness Is Important

It is difficult enough to reach wise decisions in cases with conflicting obligations when we have identified all the obligations. To judge wisely when we have overlooked one or more obligations is impossible; our analysis is bound to be oversimplified. For this reason it is important to consider all possible obligations—those of reparation, gratitude, justice, and beneficence, as well as those of fidelity—before attempting to judge.

INQUIRIES

Identify the conflicting obligations in each of the following cases and decide whether the action taken is right or wrong. Be sure to consider the requirement of proportion.

1 In studying the subculture of a particular group a sociologist must be accepted by the people and gain their trust. One such researcher is studying the people in an urban slum. She learns through their confidence that certain members of the community are involved in a car-theft ring. She does not report them to the police.

2 A Roman Catholic priest disagrees with his church on the issue of abortion. A parishioner comes to him for guidance. He does not mention the church's official position on the subject, but gives her his own moral judgment.

3 An executive of a large company learns that the company is violating the state antipollution law by dumping chemicals into the lake bordering its plant. The state inspectors are being bribed to ignore the violation. The executive takes no action.

4 A professor of psychology wishes to learn the effects of various conditions on students' learning. He significantly varies the heat, lighting, noise, and humidity of his classroom during examinations. On occasion he also purposely garbles half a lecture or repeats a previous day's lecture verbatim without comment.

5 A senator believes strongly that the country has oversubscribed the defense program to the detriment of social services. Yet he is from a state that receives a large number of defense contracts, and if he introduces legislation to curtail defense spending, he is likely to be defeated in the next election. He decides not to introduce it.

6 A very competent druggist, well-versed in the latest pharmacological studies, receives a prescription from a physician and recognizes that it is for a dangerous, highly addictive, and largely discredited medication. She calls the physician and is told curtly to mind her own business. As the customer waits in the front of the store, the druggist ponders the situation. "Should I refuse to fill it? Should I tell the customer I am certain the doctor has made a mistake? Should I call the medical board and report the incident?" She decides to fill the prescription.

7 An Old Testament professor in a Protestant seminary does not accept the school's literal interpretation of the Bible. In his classes he introduces his students to a number of philosophies of interpretation, including liberal ones. Learning of this violation of the school's traditional theological perspective, the faculty deliberates at length. Finally they reach a decision. The professor is to be fired.

8 Vincent LoDato, a California theoretical physicist, completed his calculations concerning means of controlling thermonuclear fusion. He applied for an $80,000 grant from the Atomic Energy Commission to have his equations computer-examined. After reviewing his calculations, the commission decided that they involved processes useful in controlled nuclear fusion and related to the making of hydrogen bombs. The commission therefore stamped every page of his notebook "secret/classified," forced him to withdraw a scientific report he had submitted to a journal for publication, and ordered him to cease working on the subject in question. In LoDato's judgment, the commission forced him out of that area of research.[2]

9 A doctor on duty in a hospital emergency room one Halloween night treats a 15-year-old boy whose eye was injured by an exploding firecracker. He notices the boy is drunk. Because the extent of the injury is not certain, he has the boy admitted to the hospital and notifies his parents. When they arrive, the boy is under sedation, so his drunken condition escapes their detection. Nevertheless, the doctor informs them that their son had been drinking.

10 A psychiatrist is treating a very disturbed and potentially violent man. One day the man tells her that he has recurring thoughts of killing a stranger, whom he will choose at random. He details exactly how he will carry out the crime. A few days later the psychiatrist reads in the newspaper that the very same crime her patient described has been committed. She has no doubt that her patient committed it; every detail is identical. The psychiatrist would like to inform the police, but she decides not to.

11   A hijacker is holding a jetliner and 192 passengers hostage until his demands are met. He is demanding $500,000 and a guarantee of safe passage to a country that will not return him for prosecution. The airline authorities and the police agree to his demands, and he releases the plane and the hostages. Then the police seize him and take him to jail.

12   A company president receives an angry letter from a high government official. It seems an executive of the company has written a letter to a large daily newspaper criticizing the official's policy decisions. (She wrote as a private citizen, not as a representative of her company.) The government official is demanding that the executive be fired. If she is not, he warns, the company will lose some lucrative government contracts. The president ponders the matter and decides to fire the executive.

13   When Sally's father was gravely ill, he called her to his bedside and said, "I'd always hoped I'd see you graduate from college and go on to become a physicist, but I know death is near. Promise me one thing—that you'll keep on studying hard and become a physicist." Sally was deeply moved. "I will," she responded; "I swear to you I will." Her father died shortly thereafter. Now it is two years later, and Sally is ready to graduate from college. But she will not become a physicist. She has decided to go to law school.

14   A restaurant cook is working a busy dinner shift on Friday night. In his hurry, he drops two expensive cooked steaks on the floor. He picks the steaks up, puts them on two platters, and calls for them to be served.

15 A carpenter with a wife and three children works for a home construction firm that is barely able to make its payroll. The current job is for ten houses in a new development. The carpenter is aware that the lumber for the inside walls is inferior to the grade required in the architect's specifications; eventually, the walls could warp. However, he does the job as he is told and says nothing.

16 Portia is a legal secretary hired with the understanding that all office information will be confidential. Her boss, a criminal lawyer in a large city, defends a man accused of vicious attacks on several elderly women. In the course of her work, Portia learns that the accused has admitted the crimes and feels no remorse. The lawyer thinks that the client will be found guilty and released within two years. Despite the likelihood that the criminal will be on the street again in a relatively short period, Portia does not reveal her information.

17 Claude, a college freshman, learns that his roommate and friend is pushing hard drugs on campus. Claude is not opposed to drug use. He smokes marijuana himself, though he has never used any hard drugs. Neither does he believe that drug pushing is wrong. But he does fear for his own safety, since if his friend is discovered and their room searched, his own marijuana might be found. After removing his marijuana from his room, he slips an anonymous note under the dean's door, informing on his roommate.

Considering Ideals

CHAPTER 9

How can we reconcile conflicts between ideals or between an ideal and an obligation?

In some contexts the word *ideal* has acquired the connotation of impracticality. We say something is ideal when we really mean unrealistic; we call a person idealistic when he or she produces rather grand but unworkable ideas. From that perspective, having and valuing ideals understandably seems naive and foolish. Yet there is nothing impractical or unrealistic about the term *ideal* as it is used in ethical analysis. As we noted in Chapter 7, to an ethicist ideals are not only notions of excellence, goals that bring greater harmony in ourselves and with others; they are also specific concepts that assist us in applying the principle of respect for persons in our judgments.

However, ideals, like obligations, do not always harmonize with one another. In many situations they compete with one another. Consider this case. A kindergarten boy from a poor family rides the school bus to and from school. On the half-hour ride many of the other children on the bus entertain themselves by teasing him about his plain clothes, his unkempt hair, his worn shoes. Day by day the abuse continues, becoming more and more cruel. An 11-year-old girl, sensitive to the feelings of others, notices the boy suffering in silence, unable to understand why the other students want to make him feel bad. The girl is repulsed by his appearance and is not at all eager to alienate her friends. Honesty bids her stay out of the affair. But kindness prompts her to sit with him, speak with him, become a "big sister" he can look forward to seeing each day on the bus so that the rejection of the others will not scar him emotionally.

By choosing to honor the ideal of kindness, the girl necessarily violates the ideal of honesty. Does she do right? If we believe kindness to be the higher ideal in this situation, we will agree that she does.

An interesting case of conflicting ideals occurred in the filming of a documentary account of the life of a young evangelist (now a movie actor), Marjoe Gortner. The film shows how Marjoe perfected and used his pentecostal pitch on crowds of believers. He didn't believe he was preaching a "miracle of God." In fact, he didn't even believe in God! The producers intended the film to reveal this and thus to serve the ideal of honest reporting. However, in filming the revival meeting scenes they used real revival meetings that were set up by Marjoe. Thus the crowds who appear on the screen were exploited, their religious beliefs by implication mocked in the film.[1]

Was the use of real believers in real revival meetings morally justified? To decide, we must consider whether the ideal of honesty in reporting outweighed the ideal of respect for the many sincere believers and tolerance of their beliefs. In other words, we must determine which ideal represented the *greater good* (or the lesser evil).

If there had been no way to create a set and use actors, or perhaps if the point of the film had never been made before, then the ideal of honesty in reporting might have taken precedence. But there was a way, and though it would have been more expensive in time and money, the cost would not seem to have been prohibitive. Furthermore, the point had been made in books and films. Therefore, the offense to the people and the insult to their beliefs outweighed the authenticity achieved. The producers' decision did not represent the greater good.

The Munich Incident

More than a decade ago the world shared the dilemma of West German police officials when Arab guerrillas held members of the Israeli Olympic team hostage and attempted to leave the country with them. The police were faced with the decision of how best to free the Israelis with a minimum of harm to everyone concerned. The ideal of respect for the rights and safety of the victims clashed with the ideal of reverence for the lives of the guerrillas. If the guerrillas were allowed to leave the country with their hostages, the hostages faced almost certain torture and death. Yet if the police tried to prevent them from leaving, the lives of both would be threatened.

The police tried to minimize the danger by tricking the guerrillas, gaining entry to the buildings they had taken over, and subduing them. But after this and other efforts failed and the guerrillas and their captives were at the airport, the police were left with their final plan— to separate the guerrillas, kill their leader, and either overpower the others or persuade them to surrender. (The plan, of course, did not work as intended.)

Was the plan to murder the leader justified? Had it been the first response, it surely would have been questionable. Human life, even the life of a criminal, is a precious thing and should not be treated lightly. In this case, however, it was a last resort, put into effect only after other less violent actions had failed. Finally, since it was designed to save lives, it was surely justified. The only alternative to it would have been to stand by while many innocent people were taken to their deaths. Was it, then, a desirable action that decent men could be proud of performing? No. But it was the lesser of two evils.

Ideals Versus Obligations

Frequently, ideals compete not with themselves, but with obligations. Every time a police officer takes a gun from a criminal, he or she is choosing the obligation to prevent crime over the ideal of respecting private property. Every time a doctor prescribes a placebo for a hypochondriac patient, he or she is placing the obligation to care for the patient over the ideal of honesty. Most people would agree with the choices made in such cases. There are situations, however, in which the promptings of ideal and obligation are more nearly balanced.

The body of a man who died from cancer has just been delivered to the funeral home. As the mortician begins to prepare the body for burial, the telephone rings. The caller is the director of a nearby medical school. It seems that the type of cancer the man had is very rare and the opportunity to study it more closely could provide valuable insights in the fight to cure cancer. The director and his staff, as well as the medical staff of the hospital, suggested that the man will his body to the medical center, but he refused. After his death they pleaded with the man's relatives to permit an autopsy. They refused. The purpose of his call, the director explains, is to request that the mortician cooperate with them and permit the autopsy to be made without the relatives' knowledge.

The mortician is being asked to set aside his obligation to the relatives to treat the body as they wish and honor the ideal of concern for the suffering of other human beings. If the autopsy were certain to provide needed insights in the study of cancer, we might conclude that he should agree to the autopsy. Since it offers only a possibility, and since his obligation to the family is not casual, but serious and formal, the mortician should refuse.

Consider still another case. Simone's cousin comes to her house one evening and explains that he is in a desperate situation. He has been in debt to loan sharks for some time, and has been able to postpone the due date several times. Now his time is up. He has received the final warning: Pay up tonight or die. He must raise $23,000 in five hours. It is futile even to try to raise the money. He could turn himself in to the police, but that would only be a temporary solution. The moment he was released from their custody, his life would again be in jeopardy. All he can hope for is to hide out for a week or ten days and then attempt to slip out of the country. He begs Simone to hide him in her home for a while.

Simone weighs the matters. She and her cousin have never been close. She hasn't even seen him in ten years. But the cousin's life is at stake. Simple charity demands that Simone honor his request. On the other hand, if Simone harbors him in her own home, he will surely be endangering her husband and children, whom she has an obligation to protect. The people who will be searching for her cousin are not likely to look kindly on witnesses who can identify them. Furthermore, they are probably not above harming women and children.

If there is any way that Simone can help her cousin without endangering herself and her loved ones, morality demands that she do so. However, for Simone to choose to help her cousin at the expense of endangering herself and her family would be a greater wrong. It is not necessary that Simone be certain that her immediate family would be harmed. The likelihood that they would be is sufficient cause for her to deny her cousin the act of charity.

In summary, then, in cases in which there is a conflict between ideals or between an ideal and an obligation, we should choose the action that will achieve the greater good. Where the choice of actions is such that no good can be achieved, we should choose the action that will result in the lesser evil.

INQUIRIES

In each of the following cases, identify the ideals, or ideals and obligations, that are in conflict. Examine the action taken or proposed and decide whether it achieves the greater good (or lesser harm).

1   Cibella Borges had been a police officer in New York City for more than eighteen months when nude photographs of her appeared in a girlie magazine. (The photographs had been taken before she was appointed to the department.) She was subsequently dismissed from the department for "conduct prejudicial to the good order and effectiveness of the Police Department."[2]

2   A columnist on a college newspaper writes a column praising the American Nazi Party and arguing that the security of the United States depends on the elimination of Jews, blacks, and Catholics from positions of importance and influence. Someone on the staff notifies the dean of student affairs that the column is scheduled for publication, and the dean forbids the editor to publish it.

3   A police officer is on duty in the station house when he overhears the victim of a robbery describing the robber to the desk sergeant. The officer realizes that the description fits his older brother perfectly. He pretends not to have heard the discussion.

4   Eight-year-old Tom receives a new and expensive toy from his parents for his birthday. They emphasize that they expect him to take special care of it. While playing with his friends, Tom notices that one boy keeps staring at the new toy. Realizing that the boy is poor and would be thrilled to have such a toy, Tom gives it to him to keep.

5   A young police officer is assigned to plainclothes duty in a local college. She attends classes, lives in a dormitory, and cultivates friendships with many students. Through those friendships she identifies the campus drug pushers, "sets them up," and arrests them.

6   A team of doctors has been assigned the difficult duty of deciding which of two patients will receive the next heart transplant when a heart is available. The patients are Anne, 12 years old, the only child of a laborer and his wife; and Mark, 48, an executive and the father of four children. They choose Anne.

7   An 18-year-old student, home from college during the semester break, stumbles on the fact that his father, whom he thought to be a business machines salesman, is actually a gunman for the mob. Moreover, he recently killed a member of a rival mob faction. The son considers going to the police and turning his father in, but he does not do so.

8   Raoul is a private detective. He specializes in cases in which husbands or wives suspect their mates of infidelity. In the performance of his service, he hides microphones in offices and homes (including bedrooms), breaks into homes and searches for incriminating evidence, and steams open private correspondence.

9   Two weeks ago Arthur was hospitalized for a series of tests. Yesterday the doctor called his wife in and explained that he has a fatal disease and has at most six months to live. The doctor adds that, in his judgment, Arthur would experience great difficulty coping with the truth. Today, sensing that something is troubling his wife, Arthur guesses and probes, "You're hiding something, aren't you, Martha? Is it about my tests? Am I going to die?" She has never lied to him and cannot bring herself to lie now. She tells him the truth.

10 Some time ago a man placed an ad in a newspaper seeking a young woman who would be willing to become pregnant for a $10,000 fee plus expenses and other benefits. The replies numbered in the thousands. He then explained to those who were interested that he represented a couple who could not have children. The plan was for the husband to impregnate the volunteer and then, nine months later, the couple would adopt the child. Among the reasons offered by the volunteers were the following: **(a)** a divorced woman wanted the money for a down payment on a house, **(b)** a married woman wanted the money to put her husband through school, **(c)** another married woman wanted to supplement the family income, **(d)** a single medical student wanted to finance the remainder of her education.[3] (Consider each volunteer's situation separately.)

11 A social caseworker learns that one of her clients is secretly playing in a band two nights a week and earning $20 a night. Since the client is physically disabled and receiving full welfare benefits for himself and his family, he is required by law to surrender any other income to the welfare department. Thus he is breaking the law by keeping the $20. The caseworker, knowing that the welfare benefits are based on an unrealistically low cost of living index, does not report the man.

12 Elvira is very much in love with her fiance Ethelred. Though they have been engaged for over a year (and sexually intimate for almost as long), Ethelred balks at setting a date for the marriage. Elvira is convinced that his obstacle is not disaffection, but fear, and once he can be moved to action, he will be relieved and happy. She therefore feigns pregnancy and plans to feign a miscarriage after they are married.

13   A man is elected to the presidency of a small country. Soon after his inauguration, he begins quietly to undermine the other branches of government and to assume more and more power himself. Within a few years his control is absolute. A large army and secret police force assure that his will is obeyed. Taxes rise, private businesses are taken over by the government, the standard of living of the average citizen plummets to a mere subsistence level. Protests are met with imprisonment and, in some cases, execution. A small band of men and women assassinate the tyrant and a half dozen of his lieutenants.

14   A high school basketball coach has a rule against smoking. Any team member who is caught violating the rule is supposed to be dropped from the team for the remainder of the season. Several days before the big game of the season, the game that will determine the league championship, the coach catches a star player violating the rule. He decides not to suspend him.

15   On October 13, 1972, a plane crashed high in the Andes mountains, killing almost two-thirds of its forty-five passengers and crew and leaving the others exposed to below-zero temperatures and the threat of starvation. More than three months passed before they were found. After their rescue it was revealed that the survivors had resorted to eating the flesh of their dead companions as a means of survival.[4]

16   Sharon and her friend Bill are both lab technicians in a blood bank. Sharon knows that Bill is going through a pretty tough divorce and that Bill's work hasn't been up to par. Sharon accidentally learns that Bill has mixed up several patients' blood samples. If Sharon corrects the errors, the director of the blood bank will find out and Bill will be fired. If she doesn't correct them, several doctors will receive incorrect information about their patients' physical condition. Sharon decides to report the errors.

17   Tina and Frank apply for the same job. Tina is the more qualified applicant, but Frank is the personnel officer's friend and next-door neighbor. The personnel officer knows that Frank's family needs the income badly. She screens out Tina and sends only Frank to interview with the boss.

Considering Consequences

How do we deal with cases in which the consequences are not neatly separable into good and bad, but are mixed?

Actions in moral situations often produce combinations of effects—some good, some harmful. The first step in dealing with such actions is to identify the various effects. More than a cursory examination is needed. If the judgment is to be informed, *all* the effects must be noted: the direct effects on all the people touched by the action, the indirect effects on others, the effects on the person performing the action. The emotional effects must be considered as well as the physical, and the delayed as well as the immediate.

In an earlier inquiry we considered the situation of Fred, the son of a widow with seven children, who pays his way to college by stealing and selling automobile tires, radios, and stereo tape decks. He decided that his behavior is justified because it helps him without hurting others: the owners are a bit inconvenienced, he reasoned, but the insurance companies replace the stolen property.

Fred's examination of the effects of his action was shallow. He recognized only one dimension of one effect. There are other dimensions of that effect, and other effects, to consider. There is the effect on the insurance companies and their stockholders—making them pay for the stolen items. There is the effect on all the people who take out insurance policies with that company—making them pay higher premiums. There is the effect on every citizen's attitudes—contributing to fear and anger and suspicion. Not least there are the effects on Fred himself—reinforcing the habit of solving problems the easy way, blurring his sense of right and wrong, stilling his conscience with excuses and rationalizations.

One of the earliest cases we noted was the poignant situation of the young girl who was raised by foster parents from infancy and then, at age 9, returned by court order to the former drug addicts who had neglected her. The effects that must be considered in this situation include those on the real parents, the foster parents, and the girl herself. The effects on the real parents, of course, are beneficial. They gain a purpose for living and for remaining off drugs. They can overcome the terrible sense of loss and of failure that must have plagued them since their child was taken from them. Unfortunately, the foster parents experience almost the opposite effect: a feeling of helplessness, a profound sense of loss, and perhaps a bitterness about the seeming unfairness of the court decision.

The obvious effect on the little girl is sadness and confusion at being separated from the only real parents she has ever known and at being given, like some inanimate object, to two strangers. But there is also a deeper, delayed effect. Such an experience is sure to leave an emotional scar on her. Will she be made bitter and cynical about human relationships? Will she be driven inward, avoiding the sharing of love and affection with others because of the subconscious fear that they, too, may be taken from her? Will she be filled with resentment toward her real parents and turn against them and all they try to do for her?

Each of these possibilities is very real. Although there is always the chance that none of them may happen, and instead her suffering may enrich her life and her trauma may lead her to become deeply sensitive to the sufferings of others, such a happy ending seems rather unlikely. The effect of lasting emotional damage is more probable. This most significant effect is the best measure of the morality of the court action.

A careful analysis of effects will thus cover the subtle ones as well as the more obvious. Consider, for example, the question of the morality of slaughterhouse methods. (The usual procedure is to stun the animal with a sledgehammer, then hoist it into the air by a hind leg, slash its throat, and let it bleed to death.) The obvious effect is the pain the animal experiences. However, there are other, more subtle effects that must be considered: the effects on the people who slaughter the animals and the effects on the rest of us who condone the methods used. Some ethicists would argue that everyone who participates in such a procedure is to some extent dehumanized by it and everyone who does not speak out against it numbs his or her sensitivity to other, more abhorrent forms of brutality.

The point is not whether that evaluation of the morality of slaughterhouse methods is correct. It is that no meaningful evaluation is possible unless all the effects, including the less obvious ones, are identified and considered. So it is with most of the moral issues that confront us.

When Harm Is Unavoidable

In some situations a beneficial effect and a harmful effect are inseparably joined; that is, either choice will produce an undesired effect as well as a desired one. Consider this case. Sophie has been kidnapped. For three days she has been held captive in a shack in the mountains, hoping that the ransom will be paid and she will be released. But now her captor is planning to kill her. "I'm really sorry, but I can't take the chance that you'll identify me," he says, as he unties her legs and orders her to walk out of the cabin. Hearing a noise outside, he turns to look out the window. Sophie, her hands still tied, grabs the bread knife lying on the counter and stabs him in the back again and again until he falls dead at her feet.

Sophie's act was intentional murder. Yet it was morally justifiable because of what is called *the principle of the double effect*. This principle states that an act that produces a serious harmful effect is nevertheless morally acceptable if the harmful effect is not desired for itself, but is inseparable from the good effect that is sought. In Sophie's case she did not stab the kidnapper because she wanted to kill him, but because she wanted to protect herself from being killed. Thus she was really choosing the good effect and tolerating the harmful effect.*

---

*This principle does not apply in situations where the harm that is done is out of proportion to the good that is achieved. It could not, for example, be used to justify killing a roommate to stop her from using your clothes without permission.

This principle is neither new nor radical. In fact, it is a rather old and conservative ethical approach. It has, for instance, traditionally been applied by Roman Catholic ethicists in cases of fallopian pregnancy. In such abnormal pregnancies, the fetus fails to move down the fallopian tube and lodge in the uterus. Instead, it lodges in the fallopian tube itself. If it cannot be dislodged and made to continue on its course to the uterus, it will develop in the tube and cause the woman to hemorrhage and die. Despite the well-known Catholic opposition to induced abortion, in such cases Catholic ethicists approve surgical removal of the nonviable fetus. They reason that the harmful effect of destroying the fetus is inseparable from the good effect of preserving the mother's life.

The Greater Good

In situations involving mixed effects, as in situations involving conflicting ideals, the morally preferable action is the one that will *produce the greater good or the lesser harm*. In the early 1960's a white writer, John Howard Griffin, used a chemical to darken his skin and traveled about the southern United States posing as a black man in order to determine what it was like to be black in America. His masquerade resulted in very helpful insights (published in *Black like Me)* that advanced the cause of civil rights by promoting public awareness of the prevailing racial double standard. Of course, while the study was being conducted, Griffin deceived hundreds, perhaps thousands, of people. The reason the masquerade was ethically acceptable was that the harm it produced was slight in comparison to the good.

Another interesting, if somewhat unusual, example of a "greater good" decision occurred during World War II. In the North African theater of operations many hospitalized soldiers awaited the arrival of the first large shipment of the new wonder drug penicillin. When it arrived, high military medical officials had to decide which of two groups of patients to use it on, those with infected battle wounds or those with sulfa-resistant gonorrhea. Those with gonorrhea got the penicillin. The decision may at first seem absurdly wrong. But consider the reasoning that led to it. Large numbers of gonorrhea victims were crowding hospitals and posing the threat of infection to others. Within a week these men could be returned to the battle lines where, because there was a shortage of manpower and because victory was not yet assured, they were badly needed.[1]

The dilemma the medical officials faced was certainly unfortunate, and the choice they made unquestionably caused harm. But it was undoubtedly the right choice in that situation because the alternative choice would have caused more harm. Giving the penicillin to the gonorrhea victims served the greater good.

The question of the greater good arises, of course, not only in such peculiar cases as that of Griffin's masquerade and the penicillin dilemma, but in many everyday situations like the following one.

For the first time in his twenty years as a high school football coach, Barney Bloom is looking forward with confidence to a winning season. His running back, Phil Blaster, is an athletic phenomenon. He has speed, power, cunning. Then, with practice scheduled to begin in three days, Bloom's bubble bursts. In examining Phil, the team doctor has detected a serious knee condition. His report, backed by a specialist who has studied the X rays, is that there will be great risk in Phil's playing this season. If the knee sustains a hard jolt from the right angle, Phil may never be able to play football again. Both doctors advise Phil to undergo surgery at once, but they leave the decision to him and his parents. Coach Bloom, determined to have Phil in his lineup, attempts to persuade Phil to wait until the football season is over to have the operation. Is Coach Bloom behaving morally? Let's examine the effects and decide.

If Phil plays football without further injury to his knee, the team will undoubtedly have a winning season, the coach and all the players will achieve satisfaction, and the student body will experience the feeling of pride that accompanies having a winning team. Phil himself may benefit greatly by arousing the interest of college coaches and paving the way for an athletic scholarship to college. On the other hand, if

Phil plays and gets injured, he may have no chance at a college career. Thus the possible good effects to the coach, the team, the school, and even to Phil himself must be weighed against the possible harmful effect to Phil.

The balance certainly seems to tip in favor of the coach's attempting to persuade Phil to postpone the operation. A greater number of people will benefit if Phil plays. But does benefiting the greater number constitute serving the greater good in this case? Further reflection raises serious questions about whether it does. Both the team doctor and a specialist decided that there was great risk in Phil's playing. One hard jolt from the right angle might finish Phil's career. If the sport were tennis or baseball, such a jolt might be considered unlikely to occur. But in football it is more than likely.

The fact that further injury to Phil's knee is probable if he decides to play, the fact that such an injury would end a promising career, and the fact that both doctors have recommended immediate surgery suggest that Coach Bloom's attempt to persuade Phil to play does not serve the greater good and is therefore immoral.

A Caution

As difficult as it is to deal with the observable good and evil effects of already completed actions, it is even more difficult to consider the effects of contemplated actions or hypothetical actions. Therefore, whenever we deal with the latter kinds of actions, it is wise to keep the following caution in mind:

However clear and logical our determination of effects may be, it is a prediction of future events and not a certainty. The particular set of responses that occurs and the changes in the thoughts, attitudes, and behavior of everyone affected by the action are intricate and sometimes, in some ways, unpredictable. Thus we are dealing with probabilities at best. For this reason, we must be thorough in accounting for all possible effects and willing to modify our earlier judgments as actual effects become available for our examination.

Dealing with Dilemmas

Many of the cases we have considered in this and previous chapters have been frustrating to deal with. No solution seemed completely satisfying. No matter which we chose, we were left with the feeling that somehow there ought to be a better solution, even though we couldn't imagine what it might be. There is a formal name for this disquieting situation. It is called a *moral dilemma* and is defined as any situation of predicament that arises from the impossibility of honoring all the moral values that deserve honoring. A moral dilemma exists whenever the conflicting obligations, ideals, and consequences are so very nearly equal in their importance that we feel we cannot choose among them, even though we must.

Moral dilemmas do not exist only in textbooks. They confront us in everyday life. They are a reality we must be prepared to deal with. We can never be completely comfortable in dealing with such dilemmas, but it is a consolation and source of confidence to remind ourselves from time to time that the frustration we experience with them is not a sign of incapacity on our part, but rather a reflection of the complex nature of moral discourse.

INQUIRIES

1 In each of the following cases, identify the various effects of the action taken and decide whether the action represented the greater good.

(a) A college instructor is pursuing her doctorate in night school. To gain extra time for her own studies, she gives her students the same lectures, the same assignments, the same examinations semester after semester, without the slightest effort to improve them.

(b) A physician on the staff of an urban medical center is approached by a lawyer from a remote part of the state and asked to to testify on behalf of his client, a rural doctor charged with criminal negligence in the care of a patient. The lawyer admits that his client is guilty of the charge. He goes on to explain that although the doctor is old and not well versed in the latest medical knowledge, she is nevertheless competent; the negligence she is charged with resulted from the strain of being the only doctor in a large mountain area with a number of tiny towns and a total population of two thousand people. The lawyer pleads with the medical center physician to testify that the negligent act was proper treatment. The physician does so.

(c) John and Martha, both married and the parents of several children, are having an adulterous affair. One night when they are meeting secretly, they witness a murder. They agree that they cannot report it without exposing their affair. The next day the body is found and within a week a suspect is apprehended and charged with first-degree murder. When John and Martha see his picture in the newspaper, they realize that he is not the murderer. They meet again, discuss their dilemma, and decide that despite the new, dreadful development, they will not step forward as witnesses.

(d) An English teacher in a two-year technical college has several students in his composition course whose ignorance of the English language has proved invincible. He has given them extra work and extra counseling from the first week of the semester. They have been diligent in their efforts to improve. Though they are in a construction technology program and will undoubtedly be employed in jobs that require little writing skill, the composition course is required for graduation. In the instructor's judgment, the students would not be able to pass the course legitimately if they took it three times, so he raises their F grades to D's.

(e) Regina is chairperson of her city's United Fund campaign. In her annual meeting with her staff of canvassers, she gives this advice: "Hit the business places first. Don't approach anyone who is walking alone in a hall or working alone in a closed office. Look for two or more people standing together or working side by side.

Try to make them compete with each other in giving. Capitalize on their desire to show off and outdo the next person."

(f) A senator has a bill before the Senate that promises to correct tax inequities that affect thousands of workers. However, the bill is being held up in committee. The committee chairperson is responsible. The senator, however, has learned of a secret scandal in the chairperson's personal life. He visits the chairperson and tells him that unless the bill is released from committee, he will divulge the scandal to the press.

(g) By day Sylvester is a high-ranking executive in a leading lingerie company. By night he is a modern Robin Hood. He scales walls and creeps over rooftops to enter the homes of the wealthy and steal cash and valuables. Everything he takes he gives to the poor.

(h) Jake runs a delicatessen in a high-crime section of a large city. After being robbed at gunpoint eight times in the past two years, Jake obtained a pistol permit and bought a pistol. Yesterday a man entered the store brandishing a knife and demanded all the money in the cash register. Jake moved to the cash register as if planning to open it. Then he quickly grabbed the gun hanging under it and, without warning, shot the man six times in the chest.

(i) After a young college instructor submits her final grades, she receives a stereo album from two of her freshman students with whom she has become quite friendly outside of class. The note accompanying the gift explains that it is a token of their gratitude for the instructor's presenting such an interesting and meaningful course. She keeps the album.

(j) Todd and Edna have been married for three years. They have had serious personal problems: Edna is a heavy drinker, and Todd cannot keep a job. Also, they have bickered and fought constantly since their marriage. Deciding that the way to overcome their problems is to have a child, they stop practicing birth control, and Edna becomes pregnant.

(k) A member of the House of Representatives is encouraged by a big business lobbyist to vote for a bill that is against the interests of her constituents. The lobbyist implies that if the representative supports the bill, big business will support her campaign for reelection. The representative knows that she faces a tough campaign against an unprincipled opponent. Without the support or at least the neutrality of big business, she has virtually no chance of reelection. She decides to support the bill.

(l) A company has a policy of strongly encouraging all workers over the age of 55 to retire in order to allow younger workers to be hired and advance within the company. The company pension is modest, but a retiree can survive on it.

(m) A fiberglass firm is the only major employer in a small community. Officials are aware that the firm's safety practices are lax and that assembly workers suffer a variety of respiratory problems due to fumes and exposure to toxic materials. However, no action is ever taken against the company.

(n) A major aircraft manufacturer is dependent on government and private contracts. In good times it offers bonuses and recruits technical employees throughout the United States. In lean times the company engages in mass layoffs. Employees and technicians may be laid off within a year of moving their families across the country for a job.

(o) A college receives reduced operating funds. It closes its on-campus day-care center to save money for funding academic and technical instruction. The center previously served many low-income families.

2   In the inquiries on conscience, we considered the case of a candidate for the local school board, who was running against another candidate. She had heard the rumor that her opponent gave "wild parties." As she proceeded with her campaign, she visited the homes of many voters. She made it a point to tell everyone what she had heard about her opponent, always adding, "Of course, it's only a rumor that no one has yet proven to be true." Reexamine this case, focusing on the effects of her action.

3   In the inquiries on feelings, desires, and preferences, we considered the case of the Little League baseball coach who discovered a new boy in the neighborhood who was an excellent pitcher, though he was over the age limit for Little League participation. Because the family was not known in the area, the coach was sure he could use the boy without being discovered and ensure a winning season for his team. Reexamine this case, focusing on the effects of the action the coach planned.

Determining Moral Responsibility

CHAPTER 11

*How do we determine whether a person is
responsible for her or his immoral actions?
Are there degrees of responsibility?*

I n Chapter 1 we noted that ethicists, unlike law enforcers, are
not required to answer the question of a person's guilt or innocence
in every moral issue they deal with. There are no courts of ethics; hence,
there is no formal judgment of persons. Nevertheless, as we also noted,
ethicists are interested in the question of responsibility for actions, and
their insights provide guidance even for jurists.

Moral situations, as we have seen, involve choice. Obviously, when
a person knows the quality of the action and makes a choice free from
any compulsion,* he or she is morally responsible for the action. These
favorable circumstances, however, are not always present. When they
are not, the person is not morally responsible. Moral *guilt* can exist only
where there is prior knowledge of the wrongness of the action.

The young child who sees one person stab another on television and
then, in imitation, picks up a kitchen knife and stabs his sister, and the
severely retarded teenager who, while shopping with her mother, steals
an expensive watch are not morally responsible at all. They lack both an
understanding of the nature of their behavior and the mental development to make an informed choice.

Similarly, we cannot assign blame to the prisoner of war who is

---

*As explained earlier, the idea of *complete* freedom is an illusion. Our genes and our
conditioning limit our freedom to some extent. The question considered here is whether
that normal degree of freedom is *further limited* in the particular situation.

tortured into revealing military secrets he swore to keep or to a witness to a crime who does not step forward because the criminal has threatened to harm his wife and children if he does. In both these cases, the men are acting under duress, compelled to behave as they do by forces outside themselves. In other words, they have little or no freedom of choice.

The psychopath's freedom is also restricted, though by forces within rather than outside himself or herself. Accordingly, some of history's most infamous characters may not have been entirely responsible for their actions. Gilles de Rais, for example, the fifteenth-century marshal of France and patron of the arts who ritually murdered as many as two hundred kidnapped children, may have been acting compulsively. Even Adolf Hitler, the man whose record of evil staggers the imagination—nearly ten *million* human beings wantonly exterminated and the entire world plunged into strife and suffering and destruction—may have been to a great extent morally blameless, for the evidence suggests that he was emotionally disturbed. (The question of the moral responsibility of those who supported Hitler's gaining and retaining of power is, of course, quite another matter. In many cases those people were blameworthy.)

Ethics and Law

It is precisely the restriction of the psychopath's freedom of choice that complicates the legal approach to insanity cases. Public concern over the wisdom of the insanity plea in American law reached a peak with the decision that John Hinckley, who had shot the president of the United States and three other men, was "not guilty by reason of insanity." The cries for legal reform generated by that case will undoubtedly result in change. (One possibility is the replacement of the present "not guilty by reason of insanity" plea with "guilty, but insane," which would prevent premature release from psychiatric detention.)

The legal tradition of distinguishing the compulsive criminal from the noncompulsive is not likely to change, however. The distinction is too deeply rooted in the moral tradition that it is unjust to hold a person responsible for actions over which he or she had little or no control.

More Typical Cases

Psychopathic behavior is not typical, of course. It involves a total or nearly total lack of responsibility. In most moral situations the person acting has some knowledge of the quality of the act and at least some freedom of choice. The decision as to moral responsibility in such cases depends on the *degree* of that understanding and the *degree* of freedom of choice.

Consider this case. A neurotically insecure woman constantly seeks reassurance that she is attractive and desirable. As a result, she is very vulnerable to selfish, insensitive men. When as happens frequently, a man uses her for his sexual pleasure and then casts her aside, the rejection makes her all the more insecure, all the more anxious to prove her attractiveness, and all the more vulnerable to other men.

Two of the men who have used her in this manner are a bartender at one of her haunts and her psychiatrist. The bartender didn't understand her problem. He saw her merely as a pretty and available woman. So he fed her a few drinks and a few smiling lies, enjoyed himself, and assumed that she did likewise. The psychiatrist, on the other hand, knew her condition very well. He also knew exactly what harm such experiences had on her emotionally. Yet, like the bartender, he calculated and carried out his sexual conquest. Assuming that neither man acted compulsively, which was more blameworthy? The psychiatrist was. Even though he used the woman no differently from the bartender, he understood the effects of his action more fully. He knew the harm he was causing. (Moreover, he enjoyed a special relationship of trust with the woman and therefore was required to give special concern to her interests.)

The same kind of distinctions can be made with freedom of choice. On the same day in the same area of the same war, three soldiers may perform an identical act, each of them killing an unarmed, unthreatening civilian. Yet differing circumstances may absolve one, partly absolve the other, and damn the third. The first, for example, may have been ordered directly by an officer to shoot the civilian or be shot himself; the second may have received the order indirectly and, not being observed, have had a reasonable chance to disobey without threat to his own life; the third may have killed for pleasure. Our assignment of moral responsibility would be in proportion to the degree of freedom of each man's choice.

Heroism Not Required

In considering the question of moral blame, we should keep in mind that we can be good men and women without being heroes. Naturally, it is desirable to aim for the highest and noblest actions. But there is no moral requirement to do so. The only requirement implied in the concept of morality is to do good and avoid doing evil.

A case in point occurred during World War II. Soon after the Nazis occupied Austria, they drafted Austrian men into their armed services. One citizen they called was Franz Jägerstatter, a simple, uneducated man in his mid-30's with a wife and young children. Because he believed that Hitler's cause "offended God," he was convinced that it would be morally wrong for him to serve it, so he refused to be drafted. As a result, he was imprisoned. For months his friends, his parish priest, and even his bishop urged him to think of his family and reconsider his decision. They explained that in such a situation he was being forced to serve and not doing so voluntarily, so he would not be guilty of any wrongdoing. Despite their pleading, Jägerstatter remained steadfast in his conviction. Finally, he was executed.

Did he do wrong? Of course not. His loyalty to his convictions was admirable. He was a hero. But his friends' advice was not wrong either. They and the many who yielded to the Nazi pressure and answered the draft call were weaker than Jägerstatter. They lacked his courage. Yet they were not blameworthy because they did not choose freely.

Conscience also complicates the determination of guilt and innocence. We observed earlier that people must follow their conscience and therefore cannot be condemned for doing what it bids them. Yet conscience is an imperfect guide, capable of directing one to wrong as well as right behavior. It would appear, then, that it is not fair to blame a person for doing any wrong act that his or her conscience supports. Most ethicists would accept this conclusion, provided two conditions were met: (a) the person did not neglect the job of developing his or her conscience in a responsible way; (b) the person did nothing to desensitize his or her conscience.

In considering the question of a person's moral responsibility, we should keep one fact in mind. *The moral guilt or innocence of the individual has no bearing on the moral quality of the act.* However insane and therefore innocent the tyrants of the world may be, their actions remain reprehensible.

INQUIRIES

1 For a group of people to stand by without intervening as a man beats a woman into unconsciousness and then kicks her brutally would surely be immoral. However, the moral responsibility of the crowd would depend on a number of considerations. Determine the degree of the crowd's responsibility in each of the following variations.

(a) The crowd is composed of very old men and women. The assailant is young, strong, and armed with an iron pipe.

(b) The crowd is composed of women 20 to 30 years of age. The assailant is unarmed.

(c) The crowd is a group of construction workers. The man is spindly, middle-aged, and unarmed.

2 A 7-year-old Virginia boy set fire to a building. As a result of the blaze, a 66-year-old woman died. The boy was charged with second-degree murder.[1] Could the boy be morally responsible for the crime of murder? If so, what circumstances might increase or lessen his responsibility?

3   A prominent Houston attorney, William Chanslor, Jr., was charged with solicitation of murder and conspiracy to commit murder after he contacted a professional assassin to murder his wife. At his trial Chanslor testified that his wife, having suffered a stroke that caused brain damage and paralyzed one side of her body, begged him repeatedly to help her commit suicide. He explained that he had initially tried to talk her out of the idea of suicide and changed his mind only after her constant begging to help her do so.[2] Assuming the circumstances were as the attorney described them, to what extent do they lessen his moral responsibility?

4   Five New Jersey teenagers were drinking beer by the railroad tracks near their home when they heard a train approaching. They decided to throw a track switch and sent the train careening off the tracks, down a siding, and through the brick wall of a building. The crash killed the engineer, critically injured one passenger, and caused an estimated $5.5 million in property damage.[3] Discuss the teenagers' moral responsibility for their act in light of the circumstances in which it took place.

5   A college basketball team is heavily favored to win the forthcoming end-of-season tournament. Then the star player signs a professional contract and is no longer eligible to play with his team. Was his signing unethical? If so, what circumstances would lessen his responsibility?

6   The evidence that smoking is harmful to one's health continues to grow. Now smoking is not only linked to lung cancer, emphysema, and certain heart and artery conditions, but to cancer of the bladder and of the pancreas. In addition, smoking by pregnant women has been linked to such fetal defects as low birth weight and poor general health. With these facts in mind, decide whether the following people commit any moral wrong and, if so, identify the circumstances in which each would be morally responsible.

(a) The heavy cigarette smoker

(b) The pregnant woman

(c) The smoker who encourages a nonsmoker to start smoking

(d) The farmer who grows tobacco

(e) The cigarette distributor

(f) The advertising person who creates ads to entice people into buying cigarettes

(g) The well-known personality who lends her name to cigarette advertising

7   Is heroin pushing a moral offense? If so, is the moral responsibility of the heroin-using pusher any different from that of the nonusing pusher?

8   Louise is an investigator for the Internal Revenue Service. Her job consists of closely examining the tax returns of individuals selected at random by a computer. When she finds significant errors in the returns, she assigns penalities. Because the majority of the cases she handles involve middle-income families and because it is her strong conviction that the tax law discriminates against such people, Louise has begun to feel guilty for doing her job. Nevertheless, she refuses to quit. Is she doing wrong? If so, what is the degree of her moral responsibility?

9   A high school girl accuses a boy in her class of putting his hand up her dress. The boy is reported to the principal. The principal questions the boy and the girl. She must base her decision on these facts: There were no witnesses; the boy denies having touched the girl; the girl has made similar unsupported charges about other boys in the past. The principal is reasonably sure the boy is innocent. Nevertheless, she suspends him from school. Clearly, the principal has acted dishonestly. Speculate on the circumstances that might have been present to diminish her moral responsibility for her action.

10   A major pipeline is under construction. Federal inspectors discover that hundreds of improperly welded joints have been certified by state inspectors. To what degree is each of the following individuals responsible?

(a) The owner of the construction company who paid the state inspector to certify the welding jobs

(b) The state inspector who certified the welding

(c) The supervisor of the job who carried out the boss' orders to have the work done by unqualified (and lower-paid) workers

(d) The union steward who failed to make the situation known to authorities

11 All of the mechanics at a certain garage are expected to look for mechanical problems in addition to those presented by their customers. It is understood, but not discussed openly, that the mechanic will recommend unnecessary repairs if he can get away with it. To what degree are each of the following responsible for the continuation of this practice?

(a) The garage owner who encourages these practices

(b) The mechanic who does the work

(c) The customer who, through mental laziness, continues to be ignorant of mechanical matters

Avoiding Errors in
Moral Reasoning

CHAPTER 12

*What are the most common errors in moral
reasoning? How can these errors best be avoided?*

Moral reasoning is the process whereby we select and interpret evidence and form judgments.* Like all other reasoning,
moral reasoning is open to error. Narrow perspective, inaccurate observation, confusion, and plain carelessness can combine to lead us to the
wrong conclusions, conclusions that do not fit the case or issue under
consideration. Because faulty reasoning can upset our best efforts to
solve moral issues, no study of ethics is complete without a discussion
of where such reasoning goes wrong and how it can best be corrected.

The two broad categories of error in moral reasoning that we will
examine are *errors of perspective* and *errors of procedure.* Errors of perspective occur before we ever look at a particular issue. They are philosophical errors, mistaken outlooks about the process of moral reasoning and its purposes and possibilities. Errors of procedure occur during
the process of selecting and interpreting evidence and making
judgments.

Errors of Perspective

There are two errors of perspective. We have seen both in various forms
in earlier chapters. One is *absolutism,* the view that the circumstances of

---

*In formal logic the term *reasoning* has a more restricted meaning; it is the process whereby
the conclusion is drawn from the premises.

a case make no difference, that moral judgment consists solely in applying rigid, inflexible rules to cases. "Right is right, wrong is wrong, and qualifications of cases destroy morality," might well be the slogan of the absolutist.

The other error of perspective is *relativism.** This view is the opposite of absolutism. Where the absolutist sees the need for rigid, inflexible rules, the relativist sees rules as irrelevant. Right and wrong to the relativist are strictly personal matters; no objective standard of morality is possible. Instead, what each person says is right is *by that very fact* right for him or her.

The problem with both absolutism and relativism is that they trivialize the subject of ethics. If, as the absolutist believes, circumstances make no difference, then there is little point in studying the details of cases and making comparative studies of similar cases. If, on the other hand, as the relativist believes, no objective standard is possible and everything is a matter of personal preference, then the terms *right* and *wrong* have little practical use, and ethics is without real value.

It is important to realize that there are many perspectives between the extremes of absolutism and relativism. In all of Western philosophical history (as we shall see in the next chapter), there have been many disagreements over such questions as "Is there a single moral standard binding on all human beings?" and "To what degree should the circumstances of a situation affect moral judgment?" Nevertheless, despite such disagreements, no ethicists of stature have ever endorsed absolutism or relativism as defined here. If you wish your moral judgments to be reasonable, you, too, must avoid those extremes.

It is highly unlikely that you will have a problem with *both* extremes. Rather, you will tend toward one or the other. Determine now which one that is and try to assess its influence on your judgment. Whenever you are analyzing a moral issue, be alert to that influence and take whatever measures are necessary to overcome it.

*Note the distinction made about relativism in Chapter 2.

Errors of Procedure

There are a number of errors of procedure. Most of them we have not discussed in previous chapters, though surely all of them have arisen in some form in the process of doing the inquiries at the ends of the chapters.

Double Standard   The error of the *double standard* consists of using one set of criteria for judging cases that do not concern us or someone we identify with and another set for judging other cases. It involves viewing evidence selectively or twisting it to serve our own interests. It is especially common in cases where we have a strong commitment to a certain action, often because we have chosen it ourselves in similar cases and wish to avoid self-condemnation.

For example, we may judge most cases of taking what does not belong to one according to the criteria of obligations, ideals, and consequences. However, when we encounter a case that comes close to home—let's say, taking clothes from a roommate or taking money from a parent without permission—we tend to set aside the criteria and construct irrational arguments or rationalizations to justify the action. Such lapses are understandable but not justifiable. Similar cases should be judged similarly. The fact that a case involves us in some way should make no difference.

To find the error of the double standard in your moral reasoning, be alert for situations in which you have a personal emotional stake. When you encounter such situations, ask yourself whether you have applied the criteria consistently, as you would in any other case. Look for signs that you have slipped into special pleading.

Unwarranted Assumptions   The error of *unwarranted assumptions* consists of taking too much for granted. The fact that it usually occurs unconsciously makes it a particularly troublesome error. We usually make unwarranted assumptions when we read a case carelessly and fail to distinguish between what it says and what it does not say; in other words, when we read into the case details that are not there. Take, for example, the case of Agatha's relationship, which we discussed in Chapter 7. The fact that Agatha has been seeing her minister frequently may lead some people to assume that her husband is guilty of neglecting her. That assumption is not warranted because the statement of the case neither directly nor indirectly suggests such a condition.

To avoid unwarranted assumptions, read the statement of every case carefully. Note what is said. As suggested in Chapter 7, raise important questions about the case and speculate about possible answers. Then address each significant possibility with "If . . . then" reasoning. To say, "If Agatha had a serious problem in her relationship with her husband and because of that problem sought fulfillment through her friendship with the minister, then . . ." is a legitimate approach to solving the problem. But to assume the condition to be so, without sufficient justification to warrant that assumption, is not legitimate.

Oversimplification It is natural enough to want to simplify matters. It is often necessary to do so to make sense of cases and to communicate our judgment to others. Simplification is not objectionable; it is *over*-simplification that is an error. *Oversimplification* exists whenever our treatment of a case goes beyond reducing it to manageable proportions and *distorts* it. In moral reasoning, oversimplification is usually caused by omitting consideration of some important criterion—an obligation, for example, or a significant consequence. In the case of Agatha's relationship, if our analysis ignored the impact of the relationship on Agatha's children or the possible consequences on the minister's work, we would be guilty of oversimplifying the issue.

To avoid oversimplification, be thorough in your identification of the relevant criteria. Do not be satisfied with acknowledging the most obvious ones; consider all of them. In addition, be prepared for complexity and when you find it, address it carefully.

Hasty Conclusions Drawing *hasty conclusions* consists of embracing a judgment before we have examined the case fully. Sometimes it results from lack of time to do a thorough analysis. More often, however, it results from accepting first impressions uncritically or from approaching the case with a preconceived notion of what the solution will be. Such impressions and preconceived notions are natural enough. Whenever we encounter a case, our mind begins making associations with thousands of experiences. With the speed of the fastest computer, it identifies the experiences that are analogous and presents to us the conclusions we have reached for those cases or have decided apply to all such cases. The problem is that those conclusions may not really fit the case in question.

To avoid hasty conclusions, approach every moral issue expecting to have one or more conclusions present themselves immediately and *expecting those conclusions to seem not hasty and ill-advised, but the most sensible answer to the problem.* Neither ignore those conclusions nor embrace them when they occur. Just record them and reserve your judgment until you have completed your analysis of the case.

Irrelevant or Irrational Appeals   *Irrelevant or irrational appeals* consist of regarding as support for a moral judgment arguments that have no logical connection with the issue or are based on irrationality rather than careful reasoning. There are three common types of such appeals:

1. *The Appeal to Common Practice.* This appeal argues that an action is moral because it occurs frequently. As we noted in Chapter 2, what the majority of people think or do is not a valid basis for a moral judgment. It is possible for the majority to approve unethical actions.

2. *The Appeal to Tradition.* This appeal argues that an action is moral because it has the force of custom. It is a fallacious appeal because traditions are not necessarily moral. Slavery was a tradition in the United States and in some parts of the world still is. Yet it is no more justifiable for that fact.

3. *The Appeal to Conscience.* This appeal argues that if a person believes deeply enough and sincerely enough that an action is morally acceptable, then *by that fact* it is morally acceptable. As we noted in Chapter 6, a well-formed conscience is a generally reliable guide to morality, but it is possible for a conscience to be ill-formed and therefore to lead us into error.

It is important to remember that there is nothing wrong with considering common practice, tradition, and conscience when making moral judgments, as long as we do not regard these factors as infallible guides to judgment. It is only when our references to them are *irrelevant* or *irrational* that we commit an error in moral reasoning.

To avoid irrelevant or irrational appeals, keep the focus of your analysis of issues on the obligations, ideals, and consequences involved.

Monitor Your Thinking

Being familiar with the errors we have discussed in this chapter and using the strategies suggested for avoiding them will help you keep your moral reasoning sound. There is, however, one additional approach you can take: Think of yourself as two people, an *idea producer* and an *idea evaluator*. Let the first "you" generate as many varied ideas as it wishes, but before accepting them or presenting them to others in speaking or in writing, submit them to the scrutiny of the second "you." This approach will help you form the habit of going beyond mere thinking to *thinking about thinking*. That is the habit of the philosopher.

INQUIRIES

Answer each of the following questions, explaining why you think as you do. Then examine your reasoning for the common errors in moral reasoning discussed in the chapter. Refine your position as necessary.

1 Does a man who goes berserk and kills a stranger have any moral responsibility to the stranger's family? When the man recovers from his mental condition, is he obligated to help the family in any special way?

2 Is it ever morally right for a U.S. citizen to travel to a foreign country with whom the United States is at war and to tape-record criticisms of the U.S. government to be broadcast over the enemy radio network to U.S. troops?

3 Is the concept of private property ethically justifiable in a world where there is widespread poverty?

4 Is it morally permissible to drive after having one drink? Two? Three? After how many drinks would it be wrong to drive?

5 Is it ethical for a person to smoke?

6 Is it ethical for a person to take habit-forming drugs?

7 Is it morally wrong to use a substance (for example, marijuana) for which the research evidence is not yet conclusive and which might be harmful?

8 Do rich people, by virtue of their wealth, have any special ethical obligation?

9 Do geniuses, by virtue of their intellectual gifts, have any special ethical obligation?

10 Is drag racing on the highway ethical?

11 Is it morally right to put old people in institutions when their children have room for them in their homes?

12 Is it permissible to kill animals of an endangered species?

13 Is divorce ethical? Is remarriage after divorce ethical?

14 Is it wrong for people to starve themselves as a means of protest?

15 Is it ethical for the United States to sell weapons to other countries?

16 Is it ethical for the United States to train the police and military forces of dictatorships that use those forces to suppress their people?

17 Is it ever morally acceptable to kill civilians in wartime?

18 Is it ethical for the United States to continue diplomatic relations with countries that deny women the basic rights of citizenship?

19 Is it morally acceptable for children to be used in pornographic films? Does it make a difference if their parents give their approval?

20 There are more than four hundred pet cemeteries in the United States. People often spend hundreds of dollars to bury their cats, dogs, birds, goldfish, and hamsters. Is this practice morally acceptable?

21 Many countries employ secret agents, spies whose duty it is to learn the military or diplomatic secrets of other countries. Is it morally permissible to be a secret agent? Is it morally permissible to be a double agent (one who works for both sides while pretending to work only for one)?

THE TRADITION

A Perspective on History

CHAPTER 13

*When did the study of ethics begin? Who were the
great thinkers in the history of ethics? What
contributions did they make?*

This chapter is as much a beginning as a conclusion. It opens
the way for you to deepen your understanding of the subject of
ethics, to become acquainted with some of the great ethical thinkers and
thoughts of the past, even as you continue to apply your evaluative
skills to the ethical problems of today. You will probably appreciate its
contents more now than you would have if you had read it at the outset,
for now you have struggled with numerous ethical issues yourself, felt
the pull of conflicting values, wrestled with moral dilemmas to which no
answer seems completely satisfactory. Now, too, you know the value of
careful analysis and a systematic approach. This will enable you to
appreciate the ideas advanced by the various ethicists as they attempted
to construct an ethical system. Even when you do not share their philosophic perspective, you will understand their efforts and share their
enthusiasm for the task.

Historians usually divide the history of ethics in Western thought into three large periods: the *classical,* the *medieval,* and the *modern.* Any division, naturally, is arbitrary. There are no real breaks in time; the flow of moment to moment is constant. Nevertheless, the divisions are convenient. They help us to grasp major developments more fully and see shifting focuses and changing perspectives more sharply.

The Classical Period

The classical period of ethical thought extends from 500 B.C. to A.D. 500. At the beginning of this period a rapid change was taking place in Greek society. Once an agrarian monarchy, it was now becoming a commercial industrial democracy. New changes brought new challenges to old values and traditions. The ethics of the time reflected the central feature of the society, the city-state. Thus the moral focus was the duty of the individual as a citizen. Ethics was regarded as the spiritual counterpart of medicine, its function being to provide care of the soul as medicine provides care of the body.

With values in flux, a number of moral views arose to clash with the traditional view. The Sophists, a group of itinerant teachers, questioned to what extent morality was a matter of nature and to what extent a matter of custom or tradition. Their general view was that good and evil are matters of personal decision or social agreement. Some of the more liberal Sophists suggested that all morality was a matter of convenience only.

Socrates (469–399 B.C.) was the dominant figure of the classical period. Indeed, he is generally regarded as the father of Western philosophy. He left no writings, but many of his views were recorded in the writings of his pupil Plato. Like the Sophists, Socrates rejected the idea that tradition justifies conduct. But unlike them, he believed that morality is more than a matter of personal choice or convenience. It is possible, he believed, to develop a universal set of ethical principles to guide conduct, and the key to doing so is human reason, the careful examination of beliefs and actions and the logic that underlies them. His focus was on self-knowledge. "The unexamined life," he taught, "is not worth living."

Socrates is best known for his philosophic method. Rather than teach directly, he conversed with others, asking basic questions about important matters (for example, What is justice? What is virtue?) and then examining the answers people gave, exposing vagueness and inconsistency, clarifying problems, and pointing the way to further inquiry. He was also the first to probe the relationships between facts and values, an ethical issue that virtually all ethicists since his time have grappled with.

Plato (427–347 B.C.) built upon the teaching of Socrates. Plato's writings are in dialogue form, and Socrates is the main character in most of them. Plato's greatest work is *The Republic*. He shared Socrates' view that the life of reason is the happiest and best life. For both men sense perception and bodily pleasure were less desirable than intellectual pursuits, but the two men differed somewhat in their emphases. Socrates apparently believed in enjoying himself at all levels of experience in a balanced way. He believed that nothing should be done to excess, that moderation should be the rule in everything. Plato's view was more extreme. His denial of bodily pleasure and sense perception made him a model for later religious and idealistic ethicists.

Plato's central notion was that the real world is not the world that our senses perceive, but the world of ideas. The concrete reality that surrounds us, in Plato's view, is merely an imperfect reflection of the world of abstract ideas or "forms," which are timeless and unchanging. The most important reality in this world of ideas is the idea of the Good. Goodness for Plato was a central fact about the universe. Thus the main goal of his ethical system is to gain a vision of the Good.

Aristotle (384–322 B.C.) was a student of Plato and followed his and Socrates' philosophical tradition. Nevertheless, Aristotle's emphasis was quite different from Plato's. Aristotle authored as many as four hundred works on a variety of subjects from theoretical and practical science to politics, rhetoric, logic, and ethics. His *Nichomachean Ethics* is the first systematic treatment of ethics in Western civilization.

Aristotle disputed Plato's theory of forms. There is no world of separate, abstract forms corresponding to the concrete things we perceive, he reasoned. Form cannot exist apart from particular objects, or as he put it, "No form without matter, no matter without form." Accordingly, Aristotle rejected the notion that the Good exists independently of daily experience and human personality. In his view moral principles exist in the daily activities of human life and can be discovered by examining those activities. Happiness is to be attained by developing one's potential for a life of reason. The life of reason has two aims: the pursuit of truth through reflection and understanding and the pursuit of virtue through intelligent conduct. Virtue, for Aristotle, represented a midpoint between extremes of excess and defect. (Some actions, however, like murder or theft, he saw as bad in themselves and therefore having no midpoint.)

Not all thinkers of the classical period shared the philosophical tradition of Socrates, Plato, and Aristotle. The Cyrenaics, for example, and later the Epicureans emphasized human feelings and desires and taught that the measure of an action is the amount of *pleasure* it brings. (This view is known as *hedonism*.) Epicurus, however, made a sharp distinction between "natural" pleasures, such as peace of mind and the absence of hunger, and "unnatural" pleasures, such as greed and lust, approving only the former. In contrast to the Cyrenaics and Epicureans were the Cynics and then the Stoics. These groups stressed overcoming feelings and desires and serving the demands of *duty* as revealed by reason.

As we shall see, many of the differences in viewpoint that existed during the classical period, such as the difference over pleasure and duty, have continued to divide thinkers through the centuries.

The Medieval Period

The second period in the history of ethics in the West is the medieval period, which extends from 500 to 1500. Its intellectual and social context was Christianity. As the belief system of Christianity (itself a product of Judaic thought) expanded across Europe, the idea of the citizen's relation to the state was replaced by the idea of the individual's obligation to God as set forth in the Bible and interpreted by the Church. Medieval ethics combined the classical emphasis on human reason with the idea of obedience to God's will.

Two great thinkers dominated medieval thought. The first was

Saint Augustine (354–430). In his numerous works, notable among them *Confessions* and *The City of God*, Augustine made Plato's philosophy the basis of Christian ethics. Augustine's system was two-sided. On the one side, the life of reason leads to temporal well-being; on the other, faith leads to salvation and eternal happiness. (Since this life is only a preparation for the afterlife, Augustine taught, no real happiness is possible here.) The concept of Good for Augustine was similarly two-sided: the natural, earthly side and the supernatural, other-worldly side, with the supernatural dominating. Augustine viewed man as having fallen from God's grace through original sin but retaining free will and responsibility for his actions. Virtue is possible, he taught, but to have real value it must be prompted by faith.

The Platonic system of Augustine was so emphasized in the early middle ages that Aristotle was all but forgotten until the time of the second great medieval thinker, Saint Thomas Aquinas (1225–1274). Aquinas rediscovered Aristotle, Christianized his philosophy, and made it the basis of the philosophical outlook of the later middle ages. Aquinas's greatest works were *Summa Theologica* and *Summa Contra Gentes*.

Aquinas aimed at demonstrating the harmony between Aristotle and Christianity. He taught that ethics has two dimensions—the natural and the theological. Natural ethics, as detailed by Aristotle, consists of the development of reason and practice in living morally and leads to earthly happiness. Theological ethics consists of achieving the virtues of faith, hope, and charity through God's grace and leads to eternal life with God. Aquinas believed that the Natural Law—the divine law as written in the heart of man—can be discovered by reason and cultivated by conscience. By allowing people to turn to secular knowledge without guilt, Aquinas prepared the way for the emergence of a more scientific view of humanity and of ethics.

The Modern Period

The third period in the history of ethics extends from 1500 to the present. The sixteenth and seventeenth centuries were times of intellectual

121

upheaval. The Protestant Reformation challenged the supremacy of the Roman Catholic Church and introduced the idea of each person interpreting the Bible for himself or herself. The impact of this idea was increased with the invention of the printing press and the shift from Latin to the vernacular. Finally, and perhaps most importantly, the work of scientists like Copernicus, Galileo, and Harvey turned the attention of philosophers from theological to scientific explanations.

Thomas Hobbes (1588–1679) was the first thinker to systematically approach ethics from a scientific viewpoint. Hobbes, whose major philosophical work was *Leviathan*, argued that the notion of mechanistic materialism that was central to the physics of the time applied to ethics as well. He attempted to demonstrate that in humanity's natural (primitive) condition the rule of self-preservation produces a morality based on *self-interest*. In that condition, Hobbes reasoned, the concepts of right and wrong do not exist; they only begin to exist when civil society is formed. The only way civil society can control the pursuit of individuals' self-interest and the conflict that such pursuit inevitably generates is to have everyone give allegiance to the sovereign. Hobbes believed in the Golden Rule, but he also believed that people could not be trusted to practice it. With too much at stake for each person to follow his or her conscience, Hobbes argued, the sovereign power—whether "monarch or assembly"—must ensure "the safety of the people."

There was strong reaction against Hobbes' ethical perspective. In refutation of that perspective a number of ethicists argued that human beings are not at the mercy of their drive for self-preservation. They have a moral faculty, a specific intellectual guide that enables them to tell right from wrong. Several different ways of describing that moral faculty were advanced. Some described it as *intuition*, others as a *moral sense* (a natural affection for virtue), and still others as *conscience*.

In the early eighteenth century David Hume (1711–1766) proposed an ethical theory that was in some ways reminiscent of John Locke's theory in the previous century. Locke (1632–1704) had argued that pleasure is the standard of moral judgment. Sensations of pleasure or pain, he reasoned, lead us to reflect and form views of justice and goodness and thus develop a system of moral judgment. Hume believed that the standard of moral judgment is two-sided. One part of it is objective—the consequences of the action in question. The other part, the dominant part, in Hume's view, is subjective—a feeling of pleasure. (Like most hedonistic philosophers, Hume did not approve of doing anything we wish. He believed that every human being possesses a tendency to be more pleased by benefiting others than by being selfish and self-indulgent.) In Hume's theory reason alone cannot answer moral questions. But a "moral sentiment" that chooses what is useful or pleasant can and does do so.

The Ethics of Duty (Deontology) The writings of Immanuel Kant (1724–1804) represent a significant milestone in modern ethics. Kant's main work was *Critique of Pure Reason*. However, it was in *The Fundamental Principles of the Metaphysics of Morals* that he set forth his views of the foundation of morality. Kant took issue with Hume's view about feeling and with the general position of all hedonists. He argued that moral judgments are not expressions of feeling, but *imperatives* (commands) and so can be dealt with by reasoning. To those skeptics who say that there is no certainty in moral judgment, Kant replied that it is incorrect to look for certainty in the *content of experience*. It can only be found in the *form of reason*. In other words, he believed that certainty does not come from observation, but is a product of mind.

Things that are usually called "good," such as intelligence, courage, and perseverance, are in Kant's terms only good if they are joined by the person's *goodwill* (that is, good character). It is goodwill that directs people to do what they *ought* to do rather than what they wish to do or what will benefit them. Although Kant acknowledged that happiness is desirable, he suggested that reason can never achieve happiness; it can only achieve a good will.

According to Kant, the basis of moral action is *duty*. People's goodwill is what makes them act for duty, and acting for duty gives their action moral value. The central thesis of Kant's ethical system is that there is a "categorical imperative" (command) binding on all people because it is affirmed by reason, and every rational person accepts his or her obligation to follow reason. Kant expressed this categorical imperative as follows, the first formulation being the principal one:

Act as if the maxim of your action were to become by your will a universal Law of Nature [to be obeyed by everyone].

Always treat every human being, including yourself, as an end in himself and never merely as a means to an end.

The Ethics of Consequences (Teleology)   Another significant milestone in modern ethics is the work of John Stuart Mill (1806–1873). Unlike many of the ethicists we have discussed, Mill did not create a system of ethics himself. He clarified and defended a system created earlier by his father, James Mill, and Jeremy Bentham. That system is called *utilitarianism,* and its central premise is that the rightness or wrongness of actions is determined by the goodness or badness of their consequences. John Stuart Mill's most famous work is his *System of Logic,* but it is his essay *Utilitarianism* that deals specifically with ethics.

Mill's utilitarianism is a hedonist ethics. (In other words, it makes pleasure or happiness the standard of moral judgment.) Specifically, utilitarianism states that "Utility, or the Greatest Happiness Principle" is the foundation of morals. Mill admitted that some pleasures are of a higher type than others, and he suggested that competent judges who have experienced both kinds of pleasure will be found to prefer the higher over the lower. He acknowledged too, that some people choose to follow the principle of utility because they seek the favor of friends and neighbors or they fear the wrath of God. However, such external motivations are secondary to the ultimate, internal motivation: *an inner feeling for humanity.* This feeling expresses what has been termed a *generalized benevolence,* an attitude that everyone's happiness is equal, and one's own happiness should not be pursued at others' expense.

Though Mill himself believed that the inner feeling for humanity is acquired rather than inborn, he did not feel it important to demonstrate the point. Whether acquired or inborn, he explained, makes little difference. The main point for him was that it does exist, that it is a powerful sentiment, and that in its focus on the happiness of all people it constitutes the most solid ethical standard.

Since the time of Mill, numerous ethical theories have been advanced. One important focus of this time has been on the logic of discourse; that is, on the language used to express moral judgments and the logical implications of that language. Notable among more recent theories has been the "Good Reasons" approach taken by such contemporary philosophers as Stephen Toulmin, Kurt Baier, Kai Nielsen, and John Rawls. The central focus of that approach has revolved around this question: "When is a reason for a moral judgment a *good* reason?" These ethicists hold that the primary purpose of moral discourse is not to advance theories or to express individual perspectives, but to guide conduct.

Great Issues in Ethics

As even this brief survey makes clear, the history of ethics has been essentially the story of the search for a single satisfying standard against which to judge moral questions. The fact that after almost 2500 years the search continues may seem to imply that it has been a failure. That is surely not the case. Each contributor has advanced the cause of knowledge. If the task that the great ethicists set for themselves remains unfinished, it is only because of its magnitude. They were pursuing nothing less than the ultimate basis of moral judgment, the perfect explanation of morality.

Is such a perfect explanation possible? Perhaps, but many contemporary thinkers doubt it. Still, the paradoxical truth may be that progress in ethical understanding demands that we believe in the possibility and strive to realize it. We must, like Socrates, keep speculating, keep examining, keep questioning. In that spirit we will end this brief historical perspective with some of the most challenging questions that have occupied the attention of the great ethicists over the centuries.

Do human beings have a natural tendency to good, a natural tendency to evil, or some combination of tendencies? What are the implications of your answer for ethics?

What conditions must be present before we can say a person is truly happy? Which of these conditions are most important? What is the best expression of the relationship between ethics and happiness?

Is the preserving of one's dignity or the serving of a principle other than self-interest ever a higher good than personal happiness?

Is there any action that is good in itself, without reference to the consequences it brings about? Or does every good derive its value from its consequences?

Whose interests should be paramount in ethical judgment? One's own? Those of the people directly affected by the action? The interests of all humanity? Is the answer necessarily the same in all situations?

Are some acts morally obligatory regardless of the consequences for human benefit or harm?

How important is objectivity in moral judgment? To what extent can the process of moral judgment be objective?

Is there a single universal moral code that is binding upon all people at all times and in all places? If so, how are the differences in moral perspective to be accounted for? If not, how can people with different moral perspectives be expected to live in harmony and how is the notion of progress in ethics to be understood?

INQUIRY

Answer one or more of the preceding questions as your instructor directs. Be sure to consider all possible answers before choosing any one. Try to anticipate the objections that might be raised to your answer by those who disagree with you, and present an effective response to those objections.

CONTEMPORARY ETHICAL CONTROVERSIES

EDUCATION

1   In the early 1980s a number of high schools around the country experienced problems with censorship. In most cases school boards responded to community complaints that some books were immoral or un-American by banning those books from the school library. Is the censorship of books in schools ever morally justifiable?

2   According to a 1982 survey sponsored by *The Chronicle of Higher Education*, there has been a significant increase in excessive drinking by college students in institutions of all types around the country (35.9 percent of all institutions reported such an increase over the five previous years). Perhaps in part as a response to this increase, more than half of the nation's colleges prohibit the drinking of alcoholic beverages anywhere on campus.[1] Is such a prohibition morally justifiable?

3   Under what circumstances, if any, is it morally justifiable for grade school or high school teachers to hit students?

4   A complaint from a California state senator sparked a review of the

Women's Studies Program at the California State University, Long Beach, campus. The senator charged that the instructor of a course entitled "Women and Their Bodies" showed the students in her class slides of her genitals and suggested that they imagine "doing things" with other women in the class.[2] Is either of these acts morally objectionable?

5 In education, as in business, mistakes are sometimes made in promoting a person. For example, a respected high school teacher with twenty years of service may be made principal of his school. After serving for a year in this new capacity, the man may have demonstrated clearly that he is incompetent in administrative affairs. But by that time his former teaching position will have been filled. Consider the various ethical considerations involved both in retaining him and firing him, and decide what course of action and what conditions would be the most ethical solution for the school board.

6 Once in a while a case of a teacher who has taught for years with forged credentials comes to light. Once the deception is found out, of course, he or she is dismissed and may even be prosecuted. But consider the moral dilemma that must exist for the principal when he or she first learns of the lie. Suppose, for example, the principal learns that instead of having the master's degree the records indicate, the teacher dropped out of college after one year as an undergraduate. Further suppose that the teacher is by every measure one of the very best in the school. Should the principal expose the teacher or allow the deception to continue? Would your judgment change if the teacher were not outstanding but merely average?

7 In every academic subject there are areas of controversy, questions that different schools of thought answer differently. For example, in psychology there are Freudian, Jungian, and Adlerian perspectives; in literature there are several approaches to interpretation (such as the esthetic and the psychological). Is it ethically acceptable for an instructor to teach only the school of thought he or she personally accepts? Would your answer be different in the case of an introductory course than in the case of an advanced course?

8   In determining students' final grades, some college instructors use as one factor their personal, subjective judgment of students' effort and contribution to class discussion. The factor may vary in its weighting from 10 to 20 percent or even higher. Is this practice ethical? Under what conditions, if any?

9   More than a few college professors today believe that the very idea of a grading system is punitive and archaic. Some of them, however, are in the minority at their institutions and are therefore required to submit grades in their courses. One way to do so and still serve their consciences is to give everyone an A, regardless of the quality or quantity of the work he or she submits. Discuss the morality of this practice.

10   In most colleges the chairperson of an academic department is responsible to the academic dean. If the dean should, for example, criticize the chairperson's department for submitting so many low grades in a particular semester and demand that the department review its grading policy so that it can begin assigning "more reasonable" grades, the chairperson would have to decide how to deal with the matter. Each of the following is a possible approach. Evaluate the ethical character of each:

(a) The chairperson can call in each faculty member and review the member's grading policy with him or her in an attempt to determine whether the policy is too stringent.

(b) The chairperson can issue a memorandum to the department members explaining the dean's concern and desire that the department grades improve the next semester.

(c) The chairperson can issue a demand that each department member's grades conform in the future to the normal distribution curve.

11   Few colleges today are without their experimental courses or curriculums. In their most sophisticated form such courses or curriculums are run side by side with traditional ones so that their effectiveness can be compared. At the outset of such experiments, of course, it is impossible to be certain that the experiment will be even minimally effective. Are such experiments ethically permissible? If so, under what conditions?

12 A teacher is usually assigned to teach courses with specific content. He or she is expected to select or create lessons that will impart the knowledge and develop the skills that are associated with that content. To do other than that—for example, to teach economics instead of literature in a literature course—would clearly be to break his or her moral obligation to the students who enrolled for the advertised course. Yet in subtler cases the answer is not so clear. Would it violate that obligation if a chemistry professor presented a filmstrip on chemical weapons as part of an anti-war lecture? Would it violate that obligation if a math instructor spent one class period talking about the importance of population control? Why or why not?

13 Term paper ghostwriting is surely not a new idea. But doing it on the scale of big business, with advertisements in college newspapers, branch offices, and a stable of writers, is. It is possible today to buy a term paper on virtually any subject, complete with footnotes and bibliography. Some companies even offer tailor-made papers. Is such a business ethical?

14 Some time ago a young man filed a one million dollar lawsuit against the high school that graduated him, charging them with legal responsibility for his inability to read and write adequately.[3] It seems unlikely that the courts would find the school legally responsible for his ignorance. But is it possible that the school is morally responsible? Under what conditions might it be?

15 Compulsory education, the required attendance of young people between certain ages (for example, between 5 and 16 in many states), has become a tradition in the United States. The idea that requiring young people to attend school is an infringement of their rights as citizens, a kind of slavery, is unthinkable to many Americans. Yet there are men and women, some of them respected educators, who are openly expressing that idea. They argue that children themselves, or at least their parents in their behalf, should decide whether they will attend school and, assuming they decide in the affirmative, where, what, and for how long the children will study. Consider the ethical side of the question. Are compulsory education laws morally wrong?

16 The age difference between teachers and students is sometimes relatively slight. A high school teacher could be 21 and a high school senior 17. A college instructor could be 25 and a college senior 22. Would it be unethical in any way for such teachers to date their students? Would it be different if the students were not in their classes?

17 Tenure is the permanent right to a position or an office. In teaching, tenure has traditionally been reserved for those who have proven themselves competent in the classroom. Once it is awarded, usually after a provisional term of from two to five or six years, the teacher may not be fired except for gross negligence of duty or some moral offense. The proponents of tenure have maintained that it frees teachers from fears of petty pressures inside or outside the school and enables them to function at their creative best. Recently, however, there seem to be a growing number of opponents of tenure. These people contend that it tempts even the best teachers to relax professionally and stifles creativity. What are the ethical considerations that any full discussion of tenure should address, and why are those considerations important?

18 When faced with the annual decision of how to distribute salary increases to faculty, many administrators elect wherever possible to divide the money among all teachers rather than single out the most deserving ones. (Having everyone a little happy is less troublesome than having a few thrilled and many angry and questioning.) Which action is the more justifiable ethically? Be sure to consider all aspects, including the effects of each action upon the quality of education.

19 Most teachers' retirement programs calculate the individual's pension based on the average salary earned during his or her highest earning years. Realizing this, some college presidents routinely promote faculty members the year before their retirement (whether they meet the established requirements for the rank or not). Thus the faculty members can get a slightly higher pension. Is this practice of routine promotion ethical?

20 Faced with estimates that by 1990 there will be many more trained teachers than there are teaching jobs, many college departments of education are considering curtailing their enrollments. Some critics have opposed such curtailment, arguing that it deprives students of their right to choose their careers. Would such curtailment be morally permissible? Would your judgment be the same for a public college as for a private one?

21 Is it ethical for students not to work to their capacity? Is it ethical for them to study so diligently that they strain the limits of their physical and emotional endurance? Discuss the various degrees of underwork and overwork that occur among college students and decide in what circumstances each becomes a moral issue.

22 The practice of cheating in homework and examinations is probably as old as education itself. Few would deny that it is an unethical practice in most cases. But what of the dilemma of students who do not cheat in their work but know other students who do? Discuss the moral considerations they should make in deciding whether to inform the teacher. Then decide when they should and when they should not do so.

MEDIA AND THE ARTS

1   In recent years Hollywood has produced a number of horror films that graphically depict violence. Many of these films force the audience to adopt the perspective of the psychotic killer by filming the action as the killer would see it. All the artistry of special effects departments and new technology, including filming in 3-D, combine to make the stabbings and decapitations more realistic than ever. Discuss the morality of producing and viewing horror films.

2   When advice columnists Ann Landers and Abigail Van Buren were discovered to have recycled old letters (some of them used fifteen years earlier) without notifying their publishers or so labelling the material for their readers, a minor controversy arose. Some readers and newspaper editors believed that the columnists had committed a moral offense, while others disputed that view. What do you think about the morality of such recycling of material?

3   Now that homosexuality is more open and more tolerated in our society, some advertisers are beginning to design advertisements that appeal to a homosexual audience: for example, ads for jeans, whiskey, and cologne. The appeal is often subtle to avoid offending "straight" consumers.[1] Is there anything morally offensive about this advertising practice?

4   There have been reports that the staff of a popular TV show about the investigative work of a government agency is required to submit all scripts to the agency's director for his prior approval. Any scripts that show his agents making a mistake or using questionable tactics in conducting an investigation are allegedly rejected. If these charges are true, is the agency's action ethical? Is the TV staff ethically justified in cooperating?

5   At various times one or more of the major networks have reportedly outlawed certain subjects and treatments: for example, stories about venereal disease, the portrayal of unmarried couples living together or blacks and whites mingling socially, objective examination of the Vietnam War and the civil rights issue, sympathetic treatment of homosexuals, draft evaders, and militants. Discuss the morality of such censorship.

6 The sponsors of TV shows also can exert influence over the subjects and treatment presented. In some cases they may demand veto power over scripts, reasoning that since they are paying for the show and their product will be identified with it favorably or unfavorably, they should have the final say about its content. Is it morally right for them to demand this veto power?

7 It is common knowledge that most TV commercials have very little appeal to the mind. They aim for the emotions, and use our hopes and desires and needs to condition us to buy the products they advertise. Do the writers of TV commercials commit any moral offense by these appeals and devices? Do the sponsors by endorsing them? Do the networks by permitting them to be aired?

8 Even a casual viewing of cartoon shows and other children's TV presentations reveals that the numerous and maddeningly frequent commercials used are designed to stimulate the child's normal desire for possessions. Dolls and adventure kits and games are presented in a way that says, tantalizingly, "Look how much fun you'd have, how happy you'd be, if only you owned this." Discuss the morality of such commercials.

9 For a number of years it has been widely recognized that TV has the potential to be the greatest educational device in history. (This includes not just what is presently considered educational TV, but commercial TV as well.) Does the TV industry have any moral obligation to realize that potential? If so, explain the source of that obligation and the kinds of changes in present programming that would be necessary to realize it.

10 TV news reporting calls for careful editing. Thousands of feet of film must be trimmed to fit a tight time schedule. Events that could not be fully covered in hours must be presented in minutes. Without intending to do so, the people who prepare news broadcasts can distort the news and misinform the viewing public. Do TV networks have any special ethical obligation to ensure that such distortion does not occur? If you believe they do, explain why and what kinds of regulations and safeguards would fulfill the obligation.

11 In many newspapers the letters-to-the-editor column is given more than token space and becomes a lively forum for a public discussion of timely issues. The number and relative quality of letters published for or against an issue, and even their arrangement on the page, can subtly influence public opinion. Does this power to influence carry with it any ethical responsibility? If so, what is it and how can it best be met?

12 Newspapers derive part of their income from taking advertisements for, among other things, movies. Occasionally a paper will set standards that must be met by movie ads: for example, the stipulation that the ad contain no prurient appeal. Is it ethical for newspapers to exercise such censorship? If you believe it is, do you think that newspapers that do not censor their ads are behaving unethically?

13 Newspaper columnists very often are given information that amounts to news scoops. They may be given a copy of a letter or memorandum that incriminates a government official or a political aspirant. The dilemma they must face is to decide whether to publish it quickly so that the public can be informed or to delay publication until the information is verified. Do columnists have any ethical obligation? If so, how can it be satisfied?

14 Magazine editors are regularly faced with the difficult job of appraising manuscripts submitted by writers. Often they must consider factors other than the quality of the writing. For example, a well-known writer and a relative unknown may submit articles about the same general topic. If the better-known writer's piece is chosen because it is superior, there is no moral issue. Yet sometimes it is chosen even though it is inferior. Under what conditions, if any, would such selection be ethically justifiable?

15 Film studios often buy the movie rights to successful novels. In the process of producing a film, they may make significant changes in plot, characters, and setting. In fact, sometimes the finished film bears little resemblance to the novel. Under what circumstances, if any, is it morally wrong for filmmakers to alter a novel?

16 It is a psychological truism that everything we say and do, every experience we have, helps to shape us favorably or unfavorably. Children in their formative years are especially vulnerable. Yet certain films, because of their story line, require child actors to portray mentally disturbed, criminal, and even savage characters. Is the use of children in such roles ethically acceptable? If you believe that it is sometimes, be sure to specify the conditions that differentiate those situations from unacceptable ones.

17 Is it ethical for an actor or actress to accept a role in a film or TV show if he or she finds its theme morally objectionable?

18 Much has been written about the constitutional right of anyone who considers himself or herself an artist to market artwork, books, or films whose appeal is largely prurient. Are there any situations in which the creation and distribution of such material is ethically wrong? Explain.

19 Most colleges today employ media specialists, men and women who prepare audiovisual aids for teachers. Sometimes these people are given assignments that conflict with their principles. For example, they may be directed to produce for a psychology instructor slides and transparencies that mock their religious beliefs. Is it morally acceptable for the media specialists to accept such assignments?

SEX

1   In our culture fornication (sexual intercourse between unmarried men and women) has traditionally been viewed as immoral. The reasons that have supported this judgment have ranged from religious prohibitions to practical considerations, such as the dangers of pregnancy and venereal disease. The liberalization of religious views, the improvement of birth control techniques, and the development of antibiotics have resulted in a softening of the traditional judgment. The question of the rightness or wrongness of fornication is seldom hotly debated anymore. Yet it remains a debatable issue. Evaluate the morality of fornication in each of the following situations. If the existence of any special conditions in any of the situations would materially change your judgment, specify those conditions and explain how they would change your judgment:

(a) Between two 13-year-olds

(b) Between two 17-year-olds

(c) Between a 25-year-old man and a 21-year-old woman

(d) Between a 25-year-old man and a 13-year-old girl

(e) Between a 25-year-old woman and a 13-year-old boy

2   Consider this special, though perhaps not altogether uncommon, case of fornication. A 28-year-old man is engaged. About a month before the wedding he meets an old sweetheart with whom he had been intimate. They have dinner together for old times' sake and recall their relationship. By the end of the evening memory has rekindled passion. They spend the next three days and nights together. Is their fornication ethically justifiable?

3   Some degree of sexual experimentation appears to be a normal part of growing up in our culture. Many teenage boys and girls will indulge in necking and petting (and even intercourse) with partners toward whom they feel only a slight and passing affection. Some, in fact, will on occasion do so with partners they have no feeling for. The sexual activity in such cases is performed not to express love, but to gain experience or to satisfy a biological urge. Is there anything morally questionable about this practice?

4   Sexual promiscuity is frequent indulgence in intercourse with a variety of partners, indiscriminately selected. Is promiscuity immoral? Explain.

5   An unusual case occurred in England some years ago in which a man and his wife were arrested for having sexual intercourse in their yard. Because only a row of flowers separates their yard from their neighbors' and the neighbors' children observed them, the couple was charged with crimes—he with indecent exposure and she with aiding and abetting him. He was found guilty, but she was acquitted after promising not to use the yard for sexual activity again.[1] Was what they did immoral?

6   Like fornication, adultery (sexual intercourse between a man and a woman, either or both of whom is married to someone else) has traditionally been considered immoral. Evaluate the morality of adultery in each of the following cases. If your answer depends on certain conditions, state those conditions.

(a) A married woman whose husband was left impotent after an automobile accident has intercourse two or three times a month with a bachelor who works in her office.

(b) A man is married to a woman whom he loves but who doesn't meet his sexual needs. Since his job takes him out of town two or three times a month, he uses those occasions to find a woman to supplement his sexual activity.

(c) A soldier is fighting overseas for a year. During that time both he and his wife, without telling each other, engage in sexual relations with others.

(d) A "liberated" couple joins a mate-swapping club. They at-

138

tend club parties together, engage in sexual activities with others, then go home together.

(e) A married man enjoys a good sexual relationship with his wife but has affairs without her knowledge just to add variety and a sense of adventure to his life.

7   Is it ethically justifiable for a married person to become celibate (for, let us say, religious reasons) without consulting his or her spouse? Is it justifiable to do so if he or she consults the spouse and the spouse refuses to consent?

8   Dr. William Masters and Dr. Virginia Johnson are well known for their research into human sexuality. The method of treatment that they have found effective in treating couples with sexual problems is a two-week vacation "course." The couple checks into a hotel near the clinic and receives instruction in the therapy technique, which consists of proceeding very slowly from just gently embracing each other during the first few days to intercourse later. Though the explanations are provided in the clinic, all physical contact between the couple is reserved for their hotel room. The therapists do not observe the couple.[2] Are these clinics ethically acceptable?

9   The Masters and Johnson clinics have a number of imitators. One of these is a nude encounter group in which men and women with sexual problems meet and learn to perform sexually by experimenting with one another.[3] Is this group ethically acceptable?

10   A number of other sex clinics operate more along the lines of Masters and Johnson but differ in one respect: They use surrogate partners for single patients. That is, if a single man or woman enrolls in the program for treatment, they provide him or her with a sexually skilled partner. (Masters and Johnson used surrogates in their original clinic, but ceased to do so when their use became controversial.) These partners are paid for their services by the clinic.[4] Is the use of surrogate partners ethically acceptable?

11 The problem of crew members' sex drives is a factor in two-month nuclear submarine cruises. It is solved by providing pornography.[5] Is that solution morally acceptable?

12 Legend has it that prostitution is the "world's oldest profession." Some societies have approved it, others have tolerated it, many have tried to eliminate it. Is prostitution immoral in all cases?

13 Our society has traditionally regarded homosexual behavior as a moral abomination. Is it? In answering, comment not only on situations involving consenting adults, but on those involving a consenting adult and a consenting minor. If your answer differs from your answer on the fornication question, explain why.

14 What are the ethical considerations that arise in cases where people undergo sex-change operations? Are there any situations in which it would not be ethically justifiable to have such an operation?

GOVERNMENT

1 The U.S. government continues to give subsidies to the agricultural industry. Most people have no moral objection to that practice in general. However, many people feel it is morally wrong for the government to give such subsidies to tobacco farmers, whose product is harmful to people's health. Is it morally wrong to subsidize the growing of tobacco?

2 Many people were shocked and angered to learn that the Small Business Administration had made federally guaranteed loans to a pornographic movie theater in Miami Beach and a Times Square sex emporium that features films, peep shows, sexual aids, and pornographic literature.[1] Is there anything morally wrong with a government agency's making loans to such businesses?

3 In 1982 the world learned that just after World War II, when the Allies were prosecuting Nazi war criminals, the U.S. State Department secretly smuggled several hundred Nazi war criminals into the United States, offering them citizenship and jobs in exchange for Soviet intelligence information. The State Department's action contravened the orders of President Roosevelt and President Truman. For decades after the illegal operation took place, relevant files were withheld from Congress, the courts, and the CIA. Only the FBI and military intelligence officers knew of the operation.[2] Is it possible that the smuggling and subsequent coverup were ethical despite their illegality?

4 At present it is against the law for teachers to lead students in prayer in U.S. public schools. However, a growing number of citizens believe that the law should be changed. Discuss the ethical implications of this controversy.

5 Does the United States, as a democratic nation, have any moral obligation to accept immigrants from poor, underdeveloped countries? Does it have any obligation to grant political asylum to defectors from totalitarian regimes?

6 As a result of the ABSCAM probe of political corruption, a number of representatives and one senator were convicted of accepting bribes for political favors. Many people believe that, though the senator and representatives' behavior was indefensible, the ABSCAM operation itself was morally offensive. The basis of their objection is that FBI agents posed as Arab sheiks and tempted the senator and representatives with bribes for illegal favors. Is such an operation ever justifiable?

7 Political campaigns frequently raise the dilemma of to what extent a person is justified in tolerating evil to achieve a good end. A senatorial candidate, for example, may find his staff attacking his opponent with slogans and emotional appeals unrelated to any campaign issue. Is there anything morally offensive in his allowing such methods to continue? If so, are there any special circumstances in which their use would be justified?

8 In order to gain information to help in the election campaign, members of a political party may infiltrate the opposing party. Pretending acceptance of the opposing party's philosophy and the desire to serve, they may attend the convention and try to get as close as possible to the decision makers, in person or with electronic devices, so that they can inform their own party leaders. Comment on the morality of this practice.

9 The ancient military saying "To the victor belong the spoils" is traditionally applied in politics. A large number of government jobs—at the local and state as at the national level—are appointive. Every time one party is voted out and another voted in, the old appointees step aside and new ones are named, usually from among the ranks of the hardworking party faithful. Examine this practice in light of the principles we have been using.

10 Modern political campaigns are expensive, the costs frequently running into the millions of dollars. Since the contributions of individuals are seldom sufficient to meet this expense, political action committees (PACs) representing special interest groups often make sizeable donations to candidates for state and federal offices. If elected, candidates may feel obligated to endorse legislation that benefits groups that supported them and oppose legislation that does not benefit them. Discuss the reasonableness of this feeling in light of the principles we have been using.

11 Some states have rules forbidding all executive and legislative employees to have an interest in business activity that could conflict with their public service, to personally hold any investment in an enterprise about which they might be making decisions as government officials, and to communicate to others any confidential information that would help them gain a business or professional advantage. Are such rules ethically sound? Show how the principles we have been using support or challenge such rules.

12 Elected officials are sometimes offered special considerations. They may, for instance, be given preferential treatment in obtaining travel accommodations and reductions in fare. When they take a vacation, the hotels and restaurants they visit may discount their bills. Is it morally wrong for them to accept such considerations? Why or why not?

13 Lobbying is a political institution almost as old as government itself. It is the advocacy of a particular interest group's viewpoint, usually by paid employees. Such employees, lobbyists, are registered with the government. Their job is to keep the interests of their employers in the attention of the lawmakers, informing them of which bills have the support of their people and which do not, encouraging the lawmaker to write special legislation, and even suggesting the specific details such legislation might include. Is it ethical to allow lobbying to take place? In what ways and to what extent is it ethically acceptable for legislators to be influenced by lobbyists?

14 Do rich nations have any obligation to help poor nations? If so, in what way and to what extent?

15 Whether or not they have an obligation to help poor nations, rich nations often do help. But sometimes they attach conditions to their aid; that is, they demand the privilege of influencing the poor nation's government or they expect support for their international policies of trade. It is ethical for rich nations to attach such conditions to their aid?

16 Pollution is threatening our natural resources. Every responsible person wants to protect our planet for the future. Yet some irresponsible people care only for the profit or pleasure of the moment. Does the government have any moral obligation to eliminate pollution? If so, identify some ways in which it might fulfill that obligation. (Be sure not to gloss over any moral dilemmas that those ways would cause.)

17 Most countries that have tried to deal with the problem of overpopulation have found that one of the most difficult tasks is to educate the poor to use birth control techniques according to directions (for example, to take birth control pills each day rather than skip several days). Some of these countries have found it much simpler and more effective to run campaigns urging men and women to submit to sterilization operations. At least one country gave a free transistor radio to anyone who was sterilized. Are such campaigns ethical? Is it morally right for governments to become involved in population control at all?

18 According to the Anti-Slavery Society for the Protection of Human Rights, "slavery, serfdom, debt bondage, the sale of children, and servile forms of marriage" exist in at least thirty-eight countries in Asia, Africa, and Latin America.[3] Presumably the United States enjoys diplomatic relations and trade with some of these countries. Does the United States have any moral obligation to do something about these practices? If so, what?

19 The ideological differences that have existed among the major world powers for the past several decades have made spying among countries almost inevitable. Though the extent to which the United States practices spying is understandably not easy to ascertain, it seems certain that the Central Intelligence Agency is involved in such work in numerous countries around the world. In what circumstances, if any, and to what extent is its spying morally permissible?

20 In its efforts to maintain national security, the Federal Bureau of Investigation has used informants, men and women who make accusations against others or provide the information that supports such accusations. In some cases, informants step forward to assist the FBI in advance and are directed what to learn and how they might go about learning it. In such cases, this question often arises: "How far is it ethically permissible for an investigative agency to go in contributing to illegal activities in order to gain evidence to prosecute lawbreakers?" For example, would it be permissible for the agency to provide (through the informant) the guns, explosives, and vehicles needed to commit the crime? Would it be right for the agency to permit or encourage the informant to provoke the criminals to commit a more serious crime than they had intended?

21 In 1972 the tomb of an ancient Chinese noblewoman was discovered near the city of Changsha. The remarkable condition of the body, the clothes, and the ornaments of the tomb recalled the greatness of the dynasty to which she belonged, the Han Dynasty that ruled from about 200 B.C. to A.D. 200. Under these rulers, within a single generation wars among numerous territories were quelled; all of what is now China was united under one economic system, one political philosophy, one legal system; roads were built and agricultural reforms introduced. As a result of these stabilizing social changes, the arts and crafts flourished as never before. Yet all these reforms were not introduced democratically; they were forced on the people, often tyrannically. Dissent was not tolerated.[4] Did the positive consequences that resulted justify the methods used to achieve them? Would today's tyranny be morally acceptable if there were a guarantee that it would achieve good?

22 The North American continent was "discovered," claimed for various countries, and later colonized and developed into the nations of Mexico, the United States, and Canada. However, at the time of the various discoveries, there were already people living on the continent. Discuss the morality of the process by which the continent was claimed and colonized.

23 In recent years there has been growing concern about the safety of nuclear power plants. At the same time continuing energy shortages have increased pressure for the building of more of these plants. Should the government approve further building? Do present regulations and restrictions meet the moral demands of the situation? If not, how should present regulations and restrictions be modified?

LAW

1 A number of law enforcement agencies are now using a hand-held device called a Taser gun to deal with violent-crime suspects and unruly prison inmates. The flashlight-size device shoots darts connected to wires to deliver a 50,000-volt shock. (Reportedly the device produces no aftereffects.)[1] Discuss the conditions, if any, under which the Taser gun's use would be morally acceptable.

2 Alan Dershowitz, Harvard law professor and successful criminal lawyer, has written these words about his defense of people accused of violent crimes: "I do not apologize for (or feel guilty about) helping to let a murderer go free—even though I realize that someday one of my clients may go out and kill again. . . . I am proud to be regarded as overzealous on behalf of my clients."[2] Is this view ethically sound? Is it moral for a lawyer to offer a vigorous defense for those who admit (at least in private) that they are guilty of the crimes for which they are charged?

3 In recent years there have been numerous expressions of public outrage over the parole of people convicted of violent crimes. Discuss the ethical considerations in the issue of parole and decide what direction they suggest for lawmakers.

4 In many colleges across the nation, students are required to pay an activity fee that supports cultural, entertainment, and sports programs. Apparently in most cases the student bodies of the colleges originally approved of the idea, and from all indications the majority of students do not object to paying the fee because the student government decides how the funds are to be used. However, in at least one state, legislators have challenged the idea. Presumably acting on behalf of the minority of students who oppose the fee, a group of New York state legislators introduced a bill some years ago that would forbid any college in the state university system from charging a student activity fee. (The bill was defeated.) Is it ethical for a university to require students to pay such a fee? Does a legislature have the moral right to forbid a university to do so?

5   Some states still have laws on the books that make fornication, sodomy, and even the practice of contraception by married couples a crime. These laws are seldom applied, and the climate of opinion today would surely support their repeal. Yet when they were written it was taken for granted that the state had the moral right, and even the obligation, to make laws about such matters. Evaluate that view, using the appropriate ethical principles.

6   Laws concerning statutory rape are not only still in existence but are often still applied. (Statutory rape, unlike rape, need not involve the element of force. Any act of intercourse between a minor and an adult is a statutory offense because a minor is held to be incapable of giving consent. The definition of minor, of course, varies from state to state.) Are such laws ethically sound?

7   The job of the police is to protect the health, safety, and welfare of the general public. To meet this responsibility they must obviously not only prevent any activity that threatens the public, but also anticipate such activity before it actually threatens. Many police officials believe that this latter responsibility is moral justification for maintaining close surveillance on political action groups and for dispersing large groups of people listening to inflammatory political speeches. Others disagree, claiming that this line of reasoning leads to the denial of the constitutional rights of free speech and free assembly and to the establishment of a police state. Which position is more in keeping with the ethical principles developed in the earlier part of this book? Explain.

8   Prostitution is illegal in most parts of the United States. Yet, unlike other crimes, it has no victim. Two people freely choose to have sexual contact and to treat that contact as a business transaction. Is it ethical for society to legislate against a victimless act? (The term *victim* is used here in the legal sense. In a different sense, the emotional and perhaps the moral, it could be argued that both participants are victims.)

9 Is it ever morally permissible for the state to take children away from their natural parents and place them in orphanages or with foster parents? In answering, consider situations in which the parents are alcoholics or drug addicts or neglect or abuse their children.

10 Capital punishment is the taking of a criminal's life in punishment for his or her crimes. Throughout history it has been supported by most societies, often even for crimes we would consider minor. During this century, however, more and more people in Europe and America have come to regard it as morally intolerable, even in the case of heinous crimes. Do you agree? Explain.

11 Due to the increase in crime and the inability of the courts to process cases, a practice known as plea bargaining has developed in large metropolitan areas. It consists of the defense attorney's making a deal with the prosecution—if the prosecution agrees to reduce the charge against the defendant, the defendant will plead guilty and waive his or her right to a jury trial. Plea bargaining is appealing to criminals because it allows them to be tried for a lesser crime than they committed. It is appealing to prosecutors because it spares them keeping track of witnesses for months and even years. It is appealing to judges because it expedites their handling of cases. Evaluate the morality of plea bargaining.

12 In civil lawsuits it is an established practice for attorneys to charge "contingency fees," in other words, to have their clients agree in advance to pay them a percentage of their settlement award. In many cases these fees are as high as 50 percent. Evaluate the morality of contingency fees.

13 Is it ethical for attorneys to base their fees on their clients' ability to pay; that is, to charge a rich person much more than a poor person for the same services? Explain your position.

14 The ideal of justice demands that every person charged with a crime receive equal legal representation regardless of race, creed, nationality, or financial status. However, in practice minority groups and the poor receive second-class representation at best. Does the legal profession have any moral obligation to strive to realize the ideal? If so, in what ways might it honor that obligation?

15 There is a controversy today over what kinds of conditions society ought to provide in prisons. Advocates of improved conditions suggest that society has been vengeful in its practices, seeking more to punish than to rehabilitate. They call for more humane conditions, conditions consistent with the human dignity of the inmates. On the other hand, many criticize this thinking as too permissive. Prison should be a drab, monotonous, unpleasant experience, they reason, or it will not deter criminals from repeating their crimes. Discuss the ethical considerations that must be faced in any full discussion of prison conditions.

16 A young woman removed her bathing suit on a public beach. Many people gathered around her, some to take pictures, others to scold her. Then someone called the police. They arrested her and charged her with "public lewdness." The young woman believed the law violated her rights. Do you agree? Is a law that, in effect, forces people to wear clothes in public unethical?

17 Many urban police departments use undercover policewomen to arrest men who do business with prostitutes. The policewomen dress like prostitutes and walk up and down streets where prostitutes are known to work. When unsuspecting men approach the policewomen and proposition them, they are arrested. Is it ethically defensible for police to use such tactics?

18 The most controversial moral issue of our time may well be the issue of abortion. The Supreme Court's liberal ruling has not diminished the vigor of debate. The very mention of the issue can trigger emotional outbursts. Most people tend to gravitate toward polar attitudes: "Anything less than abortion on demand is a denial of the most basic right of women," or "Any form of abortion at any stage of pregnancy is premeditated murder." In taking such positions they close their minds to the complexities of the issue and miss the many distinctions that must be made. Any meaningful discussion of abortion must address itself to at least these fundamental questions: Does a woman have absolute rights over her body or are there limitations on those rights? When does life begin? At what stage of prenatal development, if any, is the fetus properly regarded as a person? (This question is a crucial one in the law, since at the moment a person is present the issue of civil rights arises.) Are there sufficient differences among the various kinds of abortion cases to call for different moral judgments? For example, is the case of the 14-year-old victim of rape different from that of the wealthy, childless society matron? Are either of those cases different from that of the poor woman who already has ten children or from that of the young married working woman? Discuss the morality of abortion.

BUSINESS

1   In 1982 the Reagan administration proposed that an existing ban on exports of unapproved drugs and pharmaceuticals be repealed, thus permitting American drug companies to sell abroad drugs that have been banned (or have not yet been approved) by the Food and Drug Administration. The justification offered for the proposal was that it would help the U.S. balance of trade and be beneficial to individual companies.[1] Is this proposal morally defensible?

2   In June 1982 nineteen people, most of them employees of two Japanese electronics firms, were charged with scheming to steal computer secrets from IBM.[2] Such activity is a legal offense, but many business people believe there is nothing morally wrong with it, that it is necessary in today's fast-changing, competitive business world. Discuss the morality of this practice.

3   Sometimes a new invention is viewed as a threat by an industry. For example, if an efficient steam engine were developed for automobiles, the oil industry could anticipate a ruinous decline in gasoline sales. In such cases the industry might be tempted to buy all rights to the invention in order to prevent it from being marketed. Would such a purchase be moral in any circumstances? Explain.

4   In business ventures timing can often make the difference between success and failure. Occasionally, timing can pose a dilemma for executives. For example, the officers of a company may be formally obligated to consult their stockholders on certain types of policy decisions. Yet situations may arise in which there is no time to consult them. In such situations there is a good chance for the company to profit but also some risk of loss. Under what conditions, if any, would it be proper for the executives to act without consulting?

5   Drug manufacturers are required to conduct tests on new drugs for a full year to be sure that there are no dangerous side effects. One relatively small company has had a promising new antibiotic in testing for eight months. There have been no indications of any harmful effects. Now the company learns that a large competitor is about to market a similar drug. It concludes that with a four-month advantage, the competitor will control the market. The small company will be driven out of business. It decides to change the dates on its research and add four months of fake test results so that the antibiotic may be marketed immediately. Discuss the morality of this decision.

6 Barbiturate and amphetamine addiction continues to give cause for national concern. Each year hundreds of thousands of pills manage to slip into the black market and are sold illegally, often to young people. Some observers, including the head of a congressional crime committee that spent two years probing the problem of illegal drug trafficking,[3] believe that the drug manufacturers cannot be blamed if their products are put to illegitimate use. Do drug manufacturers have any moral responsibility to ensure that their products are not put to such use?

7 It is fairly common today to read of professional athletes refusing to sign contracts with their teams until they are given higher salaries. These demands, which can be for hundreds of thousands of dollars, are regarded by team owners as a form of blackmail. The players, however, believe that their skills are a saleable commodity and that they are justified in getting as high a salary as they can bargain for. Are such demands justifiable? Are they only so in certain circumstances? Explain.

8 In the early days of the labor union movement, workers were often treated unfairly. Working hours and conditions were injurious to their health, wages were unfairly low, and fringe benefits were non-existent. Today the situation is different. Some unions have achieved most of their reasonable demands. However, because of the pressure to keep winning new benefits, they make ever more extravagant demands and use the threat of strikes to gain them. Do union demands ever become an unethical use of power? If so, in what circumstances?

9 Strip-mining is the digging of shallow deposits of coal. It has been shown to ruin the land for all agricultural use. Recent experiments in reclaiming strip-mined land (for example, by dumping sewage on it) have shown signs of promise. But there is still no certain reclaiming technique. Is strip-mining ethical?

10 Investment brokers sometimes have a few clients who live hundreds of miles from their offices. For example, a Wall Street broker may provide investment counseling for his hometown relatives in upstate New York. By arranging to see them during his vacation visits home, he can claim his plane fare or car rental fees and perhaps even many of his meals as business expenses. In other words, he can deduct them on his tax return or, if he is employed by a company, claim them on his expense account. Is this practice ethical?

11 In some businesses—for example, advertising—executives are relatively mobile, changing jobs with unusual frequency. Executives planning such a change can increase their worth to their new employer by taking their clients with them; that is, by meeting with their clients before leaving the company and encouraging them to switch their business to the new company. Discuss the ethical considerations of this practice.

12 Certain hotels do a good share of their business in "hot bed" rentals—the rental of rooms by the hour for purposes of prostitution. Such hotels do not employ the prostitutes or have any direct connection with their trade. They merely allow the prostitutes to check into a hotel room many times a night, each time with a different partner. Is it moral for hotels to permit this use of their premises? Is it moral for a hotel clerk to work in a hotel in which this practice is allowed?

13 Restaurateurs may be strongly tempted to increase their profits by buying old, chemically preserved meat at discount prices or by reheating the same food several days in a row. Discuss the morality of such practices.

14 Heavy construction companies must usually engage in competitive bidding for their contracts. This practice demands that they anticipate every material and labor cost months and even years ahead and commit themselves to complete a project for a specified amount of money. A mistake in calculating or a failure to anticipate a significant increase in prices can bankrupt a company. Is it ever ethical for a construction company to use materials that are substandard in order to offset such errors or increased expenses and thereby remain solvent?

15 Employees' worth to their employers may diminish before they are eligible for retirement. In such cases the employer is faced with the dilemma of choosing between retaining an old and trusted yet unproductive worker for five or ten more years, or firing that worker and jeopardizing his or her retirement. Does an employer have a moral obligation to such employees? In discussing this, be sure to mention any special circumstances that would alter your judgment.

16 As the costs of running a business increase every year, efficiency is more and more the byword of the successful business person. The axioms of the efficiency expert are "Eliminate what need not be done; simplify what must be done; combine tasks wherever possible." Putting these axioms into practice means, of course, eliminating people's jobs. Under what circumstances is it moral to do so?

17 Book publishers are always in search of a bestseller. When they find a manuscript that they feel has the requisite qualities for success, they try to offer the author the most attractive contractual terms they can in order to induce him or her to sign with their company. Sometimes they will realize that a competitor is in a better position to market the book than they are and that the author would therefore do better to sign with the competitor. Is it ethical for them to withhold that information from the author?

18 Living in a neighborhood where a house of prostitution flourishes upsets many people, especially those with children. In cases where the house is rented, a group of local citizens may band together and pressure the landlord to evict the prostitutes. Is it morally acceptable for them to do this?

19 Employers have expressed concern about job candidates' lying on résumés and job applications. Consequently, some companies are requiring all job applicants to take a lie detector test as part of the initial job screening process. Is such a practice ever ethically justifiable? If so, under what conditions? Is a job applicant ethically responsible for truthfully answering all questions asked by a prospective employer?

20 A manufacturer received a multimillion dollar contract to supply vehicles for a city transportation system. The vehicles proved to have a number of major defects that endangered the safety of the riders. When city officials sued the manufacturer, an investigation was started. An employee of the manufacturer voluntarily testified that his company deliberately used substandard workmanship, practices, and materials. The employee was fired for giving out confidential information. Was the action by the company justifiable?

21 To guard against the destruction of their crops by pests, farmers often spray their crops with pesticides that may be harmful to humans. Discuss the morality of this practice.

22 Careless mining and timber harvesting in tropical forests can destroy entire species of flora and fauna, create soil problems, and even threaten the existence of primitive people who are reliant on what the forests provide. Yet in a number of countries business entrepreneurs are exploiting the rain forests for profit. Under what conditions, if any, is it ethical for a mining or lumber company to harvest the resources of a rain forest?

MEDICINE

1   John L. Lacey of Savannah, Georgia, accidentally spilled paint solvent on himself and it ignited, burning every part of his body except the top of his head and the soles of his feet. Despite his critical condition, about thirty medical centers around the country refused to treat him because he lacked medical insurance. (Baltimore City Hospital finally accepted him after the governor of Georgia promised financial aid.)¹ Discuss the morality of the hospitals' refusal to treat Lacey.

2   Some medical clinics participate in the testing of drugs that are still in the experimental stage. In such situations the Food and Drug Administration stipulates that the physician must explain to the patient the nature of the drug, its possible benefits, and the element of risk in using it. In certain situations, however, physicians may decide not to provide those explanations. The number of their patients may be so large that they feel they cannot spare the time to do so, or their patients may be generally uneducated and therefore likely to be confused by details. Does either of these reasons justify a physician's withholding explanation? Can you think of any other reason that would?

3   Is it ever morally justifiable to use orphans for medical research? For example, would it be justifiable to catheterize the urinary tracts of infants in an orphanage for a study of bacteria present in healthy individuals? (Such an experiment would pose no danger to the infants.)

4   Though outlawed in some states, the practice of fee-splitting is widespread in medicine. It consists of a physician's, usually a doctor of internal medicine, referring patients to a particular surgeon and the surgeon's sharing part of his or her fee with the referring physician. Is this practice ethically acceptable?

5   Some hospitals are publicly financed and controlled. Others are run by private individuals or corporations and operated on a profit-making basis. The latter, by their nature, are run with an emphasis on efficiency and a profit margin calculated in the charges for room, medication, and surgical costs. Is it ethical for hospitals to be profit-making?

6 In some cases expensive medical treatments are necessary to maintain life yet are out of the average person's financial reach. An example is the use of an artificial kidney. To pay for such treatment people must wipe out their savings and even mortgage their homes and valuables. To qualify for state aid, they must in effect be prepared to take a pauper's oath. Such a situation is obviously tragic. Is it also unethical in any way? Explain.

7 The choice of who should be given priority in the use of a rare and expensive machine like the artificial kidney can be an agonizing one. Very often it is a life or death decision for the many patients whose existence depends on it. Make a list of the most important considerations that should be made in reaching such a decision, and comment on the relative importance of each.

8 Some countries, notably Great Britain, have initiated maintenance programs for drug addicts. Merely by signing up, an addict becomes entitled to free drugs in doses sufficient to stabilize and maintain his or her habit. Such programs reduce the incidence of drug-related crimes and facilitate research into the phenomenon of addiction. Some critics, however, claim that these programs are immoral because they approve and support physically and emotionally harmful behavior. Is this criticism ethically valid?

9 Members of the Jehovah's Witnesses religious sect believe that blood transfusion is sinful. If they or their children suffer a serious accident and lose enough blood to require transfusion, they must in conscience refuse it. This poses a dilemma for attending physicians. Consider the following cases and decide whether the physician should or should not administer the transfusion. (In each case, the patient is not likely to survive without transfusion.)

(a) The patient is an adult and, while conscious, demands that she not receive blood.

(b) The patient is an adult, but is unconscious; his wife states that were he conscious he would not accept blood.

(c) The patient is a child; he is unconscious; his parents refuse to sign the permission form.

10 For a long time in Western civilization, autopsy was regarded as an immoral practice that profaned the dead. As a result of this view, there was no legal way for medical school professors and students to obtain corpses. Dedicated to their art, they frequently either dug up recently buried corpses or paid others to do so, without the consent of the dead person's relatives. Were it not for this ghoulish practice, medical science would surely not have developed nearly so extensively or rapidly as it has. Was the practice ethically justifiable?

11 Psychologists and psychiatrists often deal with cases of impotence. As part of their treatment of unmarried patients, they may prescribe a visit to a prostitute. This practice is illegal in most states. Is it also immoral?

12 About one baby out of every six hundred born in the United States is mongoloid. Such children have slanted eyes, broad noses, and I.Q.'s of about 30. Many are born with fatal physical defects: Parts of vital organs may be missing, the intestines may be blocked, or the heart may not function properly. Often surgery is necessary if they are to survive beyond the first few days of life. The parents must face the question of whether to permit such surgery and save the child, which would mean spending thousands of dollars for special care and education (and in some cases, for institutionalization), or whether to withhold permission and let the child die. Anthony Shaw, an associate professor of surgery and pediatrics at the University of Virginia Medical Center, cites the conflicting views of surgeons over the morality of withholding permission.[2] One is that in any such situation, not operating would be tantamount to murder. Another is that operating would be wrong because "the emotional and financial costs involved are too great to justify the procedure." The third view, Shaw's own, is more flexible. He believes that the circumstances, which can be fully evaluated only by the parents, may make operation right in one case but wrong in another. Which position is most ethically sound and why?

13 Serious accidents can leave their victims comatose for months and even years. The longer the coma lasts, the less chance the person has of regaining consciousness. There are people who live in that state, cared for at considerable expense in hospitals or nursing homes, unable to relate to their loved ones, unaware that they are technically alive. Such cases inevitably raise the question of euthanasia (mercy killing). Merely by injecting a poisonous substance into a vein, a doctor or nurse could spare the victim his limbo of near-life and grant him a painless death. Would it be ethically justifiable to do so in such a situation? Would it be justifiable in any other situation?

14 The development of organ transplant techniques has increased the need for donors. Since organs such as the heart can only be (ethically) removed from persons who have just died, the age-old question "When does death occur?" has taken on new importance. Some medical authorities say it occurs when the heart has stopped beating and fails to respond to massage or chemical stimulants. Others say death occurs when the central nervous system has ceased to function (that is, when reflexes cannot be aroused). One authority, Hans Jonas, however, reasons as follows: *"Since we do not know the exact borderline between life and death*, nothing less than the maximum definition of death will do—brain death plus heart death plus any other indication that may be pertinent—before final violence [for example, the taking of an organ for transplant purposes] is allowed to be done."[3] Keeping in mind that Jonas's conclusion would reduce the number of transplant donors, evaluate his reasoning in light of the principles in this book.

15 The same medicine purchased under the generic name costs considerably less than when purchased under a brand name. Yet doctors often prescribe by brand name. Is it ethical for them to do so?

16 According to at least one authority, a number of doctors around the country are prescribing amphetamines rather freely for their patients. Is this practice ethical? In answering, consider that amphetamines are habit-forming and can produce symptoms of schizophrenia and paranoia.[4]

17 Hospital workers in a large urban area feel that they are not being paid enough and that their fringe benefits are substandard. They decide to strike. Taking advantage of the special need for their services during holiday periods, they plan the strike to take place ten days before a major holiday weekend. This timing, they expect, will pressure hospital management to meet their demands. Discuss the morality of this strike.

18 Abortion may be the most controversial moral issue of our time. Countless books and articles have been written about it. Laws have banned it and permitted it. Thoughtful and informed people continue to debate the matter. Identify the moral considerations that any responsible analysis of this issue must include.

SCIENCE

1   The site of an old Cherokee Indian Village in Tennessee was about to be flooded in the process of creating a new Tennessee Valley Authority dam. In an effort to find and preserve the artifacts of Indian civilization known to be buried in the area, archaeologists from a University of Tennessee museum undertook extensive digging. The Cherokee Indians objected to the dam because it represented "flooding a whole race of people's history and heritage off the map." They also objected to the digging because in their view it desecrated the graves of their ancestors.[1] Evaluate the morality both of the government's building the dam and of the archaeological team's digging the area.

2   Some years ago a study was made to determine the psychological effects of oral contraceptives. About four hundred poor women, who had sought family planning assistance, participated. Most of the women were Mexican-Americans with large families. Some of the women were given oral contraceptives; others were given dummy pills with no birth control chemical. As a result, six of the women in the "dummy group" became pregnant.[2] Evaluate the ethical character of the study.

3   It is now possible for a woman whose husband is sterile to be artificially inseminated with the semen of a donor. Is this practice ethical? If it is in some circumstances but not in others, be sure to explain those circumstances carefully.

4   It will someday be possible for a woman whose ovaries cannot produce an ovum to receive one from a donor. Would this practice be ethical? If so, under what conditions?

5   The time is 1990. A businesswoman wants to have a baby but can't spare the nine months. She goes to a laboratory and, following a new scientific technique, "conceives" a baby from her ovum and her husband's sperm. Then she has the fertilized egg implanted in another

162

woman's uterus. Nine months later, the baby safely delivered, she pays the woman for her "labor." Comment on the morality of this procedure.

6 Much of what we hear about the advent of test-tube babies still has the ring of science fiction to it. Yet in all probability a successful technique for conceiving and nurturing a human fetus in an artificial uterus is certain to be developed. Naturally such an achievement will be preceded by many fumbling, partially successful efforts. Many scientists, in other words, will be creating human embryos, sustaining them for a time—for a few days at first, and then as their techniques become refined, for a few weeks, three months, seven months. Most, perhaps all, of these embryos and fetuses will be destroyed when they have served their scientific purpose. Is such creation of fetuses ethical? Is their destruction ethical?

7 A scientific organization wishes to conduct research on the effects of ultrasound on human beings. It secures the permission of a local hospital to bombard fetuses that are about to be legally aborted and then to autopsy them after abortion. Is such an experiment ethical?

8 A famous experiment by Yale University's Dr. Jose Delgado dramatized the effectiveness of electrical stimulation of the brain (ESB) as a means of controlling behavior. He "wired" the brain of a fighting bull and demonstrated that merely by pushing a button and sending an electrical current coursing into the animal's brain, he could stop it in the middle of an enraged charge. He also showed that repeated stimulation diminished the bull's natural aggressiveness. Similar experiments have shown that the same effects occur on humans. For example, people given to uncontrollable fits of rage can have their brains so wired that, when they feel a seizure coming on, they need only press a button to be instantly calmed. Is the wiring operation ethical if the patient consents to it? Are there any circumstances in which it would be ethical even if he or she did not consent?

9 Another area of research that shows potential for control of behavior is chemical stimulation of the brain (CSB). Tiny tubes can be placed in strategic parts of the brain and chemicals secreted on a timed-release basis. A given emotional state can thus be maintained in the patient independent of his or her control. Following are some of the uses CSB might be put to. Examine the morality of each:

(a) Candidates for high public office or for appointive positions such as the President's cabinet could be required to submit to CSB so that the public could be assured no conscious or subconscious aggressiveness in its officials would lead the country into war.

(b) Persons convicted of violent crimes could be treated to ensure that they would not act violently again.

(c) Students who have very short attention spans that hamper their learning or negative attitudes toward teachers and the learning process could be treated to increase their learning potential.

(d) Newborn children could be so treated that they would not be susceptible to propaganda or to the promptings of fanatics.

10 Throughout history it has been the practice in many countries to use convicts in scientific experiments. The practice continues today. If, for example, researchers develop a chemical that preliminary exploratory work indicates will cure a fatal disease, they may seek volunteers from prison populations, administer the chemical to them, and determine its effects on the human body. Or a psychologist studying the effects of extreme variations in climate on the human body may subject consenting prisoners to such variations and test their reactions. Though such experiments are usually very carefully designed to minimize the risk to participants, an element of risk always remains. The participants may become ill or even die of unexpected physical or emotional effects. Because of this danger, volunteers are usually promised special privileges during the course of the experiment and even a reduction of their prison sentences. In cases involving unusual risk, full pardons may be promised. Is it ethical to use prisoners for such experiments? Is it ethical to provide such inducements to volunteers?

11   Sometimes medical school professors encourage their students to volunteer for research experiments. (Student volunteers are used just as prisoner volunteers are, though without rewards—except, of course, the emotional satisfaction of having contributed to progress.) Is such encouragement ethically permissible?

12   Some geneticists, notably Dr. Herman J. Muller, a Nobel Prize winner, have proposed that sperm banks solicit donations of sperm cells from carefully selected men whose lives had shown unusual mental, emotional, or physical gifts. Couples would then be able to select the genetic material of their choice and therefore produce a child endowed with the heredity that matched their ideals. Evaluate the morality of this proposal.

13   The transplants of organs such as the heart and the kidneys have been shown to be possible. Before too long, scientists assure us, the transplant of the brain will also be a reality. Will such an operation ever be ethically justifiable? In answering, be sure to consider the various activities of the brain and their influence on personal identity.

14   *Cloning* is making carbon copies, genetically exact duplicates, of individual organisms. It was first developed in the early 1960s by Cornell University Professor F. C. Steward, who agitated carrot root cells, causing them to divide and multiply. Eventually he was able to prompt a single cell to develop into a fully-grown carrot plant. Later, Professor John Gordon of Oxford University achieved similar results with a frog. The possibilities of using this technique with animals—for example, beef cattle—and with humans are very real. There are, of course, technical difficulties that must be solved. But no knowledgeable person doubts that these will eventually be solved. When this happens it will be possible to scrape a cell from a person's hand and create an exact copy of that person, a flesh and blood replica with the same genetic traits. (The procedure would be to destroy the nucleus of an egg cell from a donor and insert in its place the nucleus of any cell of the person to be copied. After being nurtured in a nutrient medium for several days, the egg would then be implanted in the uterine wall of the mother.) Thus there could be an unlimited supply of Bette Davises, John Glenns, Kareem Abdul-Jabbars. Since heredity is only part of the influence on people, their behavior and interests would not necessarily be the same. But their appearance and basic capacities would be. Discuss the morality of cloning.

15 Hans Jonas has suggested that in considering the ethical character of scientific experiments we should distinguish between "averting a disaster" and "prompting a good."[3] In the first, where the goal is *saving* society, Jonas concedes that extraordinary means may be used. However, in the latter, where the goal, *improving society*, is less urgent, such means may not be tolerated. According to Jonas,

> Our descendants have a right to be left an unplundered planet. They do not have a right to miracle cures. We have sinned against them if by our doing we have destroyed their inheritance—which we are doing at full blast; we have not sinned against them if by the time they come around arthritis has not yet been conquered (unless by sheer neglect). And generally, in the matter of progress, as humanity had no claim on a Newton, a Michelangelo, or a St. Francis to appear, and no right to the blessings of their unscheduled deeds, so progress, with all our methodical labor for it, cannot be budgeted in advance and its fruits received as a due. Its coming about at all and its turning out for good (of which we can never be sure) must rather be regarded as something akin to grace.

Would Jonas' distinctions be helpful in evaluating any of the preceding cases (1–14) in this section? Explain.

16 David D. Rutstein made the following assertions about the selection and design of scientific experiments. Do you agree with these assertions? Do they have special application to any of the preceding cases (1–14)? Explain.

(a) ". . . In selecting a question for human experimentation, the expectation of benefit to the subject and to mankind must clearly far exceed the risk to the human subject."[4]

(b) "It may be accepted as a maxim that a poorly or improperly designed study involving human subjects—one that could not possibly yield scientific facts (that is, reproducible observations) relevant to the question under study—is by definition unethical . . . Any risk to the patient, however small, cannot be justified. In essence, the scientific validity of a study on human beings is in itself an ethical principle."[5]

17 Given the threat that nuclear weapons pose for humanity, is it ever morally acceptable for scientists to engage in research and development work on such weapons? Discuss the conditions, if any, under which it would be acceptable.

WAR

1 Israel's invasion of Lebanon in 1982 was conducted to root out the PLO forces that had been responsible for terrorist attacks on Israelis. The Israeli action was controversial because the Lebanese people who were killed or whose homes were destroyed during the invasion had done nothing to Israel. Some people argue that it is always immoral for a nation to invade a neighboring nation that has given no provocation. Others disagree, claiming (as the Israelis did) that an invasion is justified if there is no other way to overcome terrorist forces who have set up headquarters there. Which position do you endorse and why?

2 Is it morally wrong for the government to prosecute a person who fails to register for the draft?

3 A growing number of people today believe that war is always wrong, that no circumstances ever justify one nation's taking up arms against another. Is the view ethically sound? In answering, be sure to comment on the questions of a country's defending itself against aggression and of a strong country's coming to the aid of a weak country that has been attacked unjustly.

4 A soldier's thinking about war may change during his service. For example, after experiencing his first real battle and seeing human beings lying dead or in the agony of pain, a soldier might be prompted to embrace pacifism and request discharge or transfer to a noncombat unit. Such a request would not be looked on favorably by his superiors and would usually be denied. Since the man had accepted training as a combat soldier, they would reason, he would be obligated to finish his term of service. Is this reasoning morally sound? Would it be morally acceptable for the soldier to continue fighting, even though he objected to it on principle?

5 A career officer may not object to war in general, but may, after much observation and evaluation, conclude that his or her country's involvement in the particular war of the moment is morally unjustifiable. Would any circumstances make it morally acceptable for the officer to continue to serve in that war? Explain.

6 In the United States, Congress alone has the power to declare or end a war. The President, as commander in chief of the armed forces, therefore has the legal obligation to keep Congress informed of his dealings with foreign powers, particularly during wartime. Are there any circumstances in which it would be ethically justifiable for the President to conduct secret talks with the enemy and with interested third parties in order to set up the conditions for peace? Would any circumstance justify the President's lying to Congress? Explain.

7 Over the centuries the experience of war has produced many "conventions," humane rules to limit the devastation and suffering that conflict brings. One of the foremost of these rules is that only military targets will be attacked: that civilian population centers that contain no significant deposit of war supplies and machinery will be spared. However, during World War II the United States firebombed the German city of Dresden, dropping thousands of tons of TNT and killing more than 100,000 noncombatants. That target was allegedly selected precisely because it was a civilian target and its elimination would demoralize the enemy and, as a result, shorten the war. Discuss the morality of the bombing of Dresden.

8 The dropping of atomic bombs on the Japanese cities of Hiroshima and Nagasaki was approved because it would make a land invasion of Japan unnecessary and prevent the loss of tens of thousands of American troops. (A land invasion would have destroyed numerous Japanese towns and taken countless Japanese lives, as well.) Yet the bombings leveled two cities, killed well over 100,000 people, and caused the agony of radiation burns to thousands of others and genetic damage to their offspring. Discuss the morality of dropping the atomic bombs.

9 Guerrilla warfare consists of terrorization tactics designed to demoralize the enemy and thereby achieve the enemy's defeat.

Through threats of harm to themselves and their loved ones, civilians are coerced to harbor guerrillas in their villages and to aid them in acts of sabotage. Is it ever ethically justifiable to conduct guerrilla warfare? If so, in what situations?

10 During the Vietnam War reports from North Vietnam claimed that the United States was engaging in the deliberate bombing of the 2,500-mile network of dikes that protect countless farms and villages from the flooding of the Red River. The U.S. government denied the charges, explaining that any such bombings that may have occurred were accidental. Were such bombing done deliberately, it would have had several obvious consequences. It would have threatened the food supply, the homes and factories, and the lives of tens of thousands of civilians. It would also have hindered the North Vietnamese war effort, prompted them to be less demanding at the conference table, and perhaps hastened the end of the war. Would it have been a morally acceptable policy?

11 The argument that has underlain many of the wartime atrocities that people have perpetrated is "they started the war, so we're justified in using whatever means are necessary to finish it." A variation of this, which is used whenever it is not clear who "started it," is "they violated the human convention first so we have a right to also." It was used in the Indian wars (though objective scholarship has shown that much of the savagery that was attributed to the Indians was done first by whites). It was used during World War I and World War II. It was used in Korea and Vietnam. Evaluate the argument from an ethical standpoint.

12 The practice of torturing prisoners to obtain military information is as old as the art of war. Captives are beaten, subjected to electric shock, made to go without sleep for days, and given little or no food. Is such treatment ever justifiable? Be sure to consider unusual situations as well as more common ones; for example, the situation in which the captive is a guerrilla who, there is reason to believe, may have poisoned a city's water supply or placed a time bomb in a public area.

170

13 Anticipating the possibility that their soldiers may one day be captured by the enemy, some modern armies include in their basic training exposure to torture techniques. That is, they subject their own troops to mild forms of torture in order that they may learn how to resist torture. Is this practice justifiable morally? If you believe it is justifiable only under certain conditions, specify the conditions.

14 Like every aspect of modern existence, the waging of war is largely technological. Among the weapons now available are bombs that seek out groups of people (presumably the enemy) through heat sensors, and fragmentation bombs that burrow into the earth to await detonation when someone (presumably an enemy soldier) steps on them. Are such weapons morally legitimate in war? Explain.

15 The Pentagon has spent millions of dollars for research into "electro-optical warfare." The device that was the subject of much of this research is the versatile laser beam. It has the potential for use as an ICBM interceptor. Traveling at the speed of light, it can catch and explode the most sophisticated missiles an enemy might launch. It can ignite wooden targets miles away and can instantly burn out the eyes of anyone who looks directly into it. When aimed at an enemy soldier, it can unerringly burn a fatal hole in his body.[1] Is research into the use of such weapons ethically justifiable? Is the use of such weapons any less moral than the use of guns?

16 If such weapons as those discussed in the preceding question become a reality, would it be morally wrong to work in a company that makes them? To hold stock in such a company?

17 Another avenue of potential for warfare is meteorology. Scientists agree that we presently have or will soon have the technological ability to change the earth's temperature, cause tidal waves, create "holes" in the atmosphere that would permit harmful solar radiation to shower selected geographical areas, and create precipitation where we wish. (There have been reports that the last potential was actually realized by the United States in the Vietnam War to impede travel along the Ho Chi Minh trail.) Comment on such practices from an ethical standpoint.

AFTERWORD

A Suggestion for Further Study

Many times students will complete an enjoyable college course with a firm resolution to continue studying the subject on their own. Yet somehow, despite their good intentions and their genuine interest in the subject, they never get around to keeping their resolution. The reason is usually that they think of further study in terms of buying or borrowing a book. But which book? They don't know and they don't know how to find out because they are not sure whether they want a general history of the subject, a discussion of one particular aspect of it, a treatment of contemporary issues, or a biography of a famous contributor to the subject.

If you are now making such a resolution about the subject of ethics, here is how to be sure you keep that resolution. Make it very modest. Instead of resolving to buy or borrow a book, resolve to read a single *article* the next time you visit the library and have a few spare minutes.

To find the article you want, you needn't search through the magazine index or browse through current periodicals. All you have to do is consult the *Encyclopedia of Philosophy*.

Published in eight volumes by Macmillan and The Free Press, the *Encyclopedia of Philosophy* contains numerous authoritative articles on all aspects of ethics (as well as articles on other philosophical disciplines). You may wish to begin with an article about one of the great issues in ethics—for example, "Conscience," or "The Good" or "Happiness." Or perhaps you would rather learn more about the schools of ethical thought. In that case, you would choose an article like "Deontological Ethics," "Teleological Ethics," "Hedonism," or "Utilitarianism." You will also find individual articles on all the great ethicists from Socrates to the present. Finally, you might choose to read one or both of the two detailed survey articles, "Ethics, History of" and "Ethics, Problems of."

There is an additional advantage to this approach to independent study in ethics. At the end of each article is a bibliography of works that provide even more specific and detailed information on the subject of the article. Most of these books will either be on the shelves of your college library or obtainable through interlibrary loan. If you have the time to read one or more books, you can pick them up or order them while you are in the library. If your schedule does not afford you that kind of time, you can at least return again and again to the *Encyclopedia of Philosophy*, thus ensuring that your knowledge of ethics will continue to grow long after your formal course in ethics has ended.

APPENDIX

Writing About Moral Issues

The principles that apply to writing about moral issues are the same ones that apply to all expository writing. However, because moral discourse often involves the expression of ideas that readers may be inclined to disagree with, sometimes vigorously, there is a special reason to express the principles thoroughly and thoughtfully. In this kind of writing, where persuasion is the main intention, there is no margin for carelessness.

The fundamental principles may be stated briefly: The main idea must be clear, the relationships between sentences and paragraphs must be coherent, the space assigned to each part of the presentation must match the relative importance of that part (in relation to other parts), all interpretations and judgments must be sufficiently explained and supported to satisfy the critical reader, and the overall style must be readable (if possible, *pleasurable* to read).

Let's examine each of these principles closely, concentrating on the strategies that will help you achieve it in your writing.

How to Make the Main Idea Clear
(CLAR)

In most papers about ethics the main idea will be the writer's judgment of the morality of the action that is being considered. Lack of clarity in the main idea usually occurs because the writer began without knowing exactly what he or she wanted to say, hoping to discover the idea in the process of writing. Sadly, the writer will often reach the end of the piece without having made that discovery. Even when the writer is lucky enough to do so, perhaps midway through the piece, by that point he or she has usually confused the reader and made one or more statements that are inconsistent with the main idea. In such cases the reader is apt to dismiss the writer as confused or uninformed. You can prevent this development in your own efforts by scrupulously following two simple strategies:

1. *Begin writing only after you have determined exactly what you are going to say; that is, after you have decided what your judgment is and what basis you have for making it.* This strategy does not rule out "brainstorming" and "freewriting."* In fact, it is perfectly compatible with them, as long as they are used as *preliminaries* to formal writing and not as formal writing itself. If you use brainstorming and freewriting—and they are well worth using—be sure to resist the temptation to deceive yourself by saying, "These notes look good enough to submit as they are; I'll just copy them over to make them neater and the job will be done." Instead, when you have finished producing your ideas, review the ideas and ask yourself what you really want to say.

*These techniques consist of letting your mind range over the subject (or forcing it to do so), without evaluating the ideas that occur, or screening any out, or attempting to organize them in any way, or correcting your errors. The aim of such techniques is to produce a large body of ideas from which you may *later* select the best ones, the ones you wish to include in your final piece of writing. The principle that underlies brainstorming and freewriting is that ideas and associations will flow best when they are uninterrupted by analysis and judgment.

2. *Experiment with different ways of expressing your main idea and select the best one.* Don't settle for your first way of expressing the idea. That way may lack the qualifications and the exactness that reasonableness demands. As you try different ways of expressing the idea, look at the related ideas and evidence that your preliminary work produced. Ask which way of expressing the thought is most reasonable and best reflects the relevant moral principles that are involved. Ask, too, what your readers' reactions are likely to be, particularly what objections they might have. Refine your statement of the idea in light of these considerations.

How to Keep Sentences and Paragraphs Coherent (COH)

You will already have taken one step toward achieving coherence when you determine your main idea. The very fact that you have that idea before beginning will provide a center to your piece of writing, something to relate the other parts to. Yet there are specific strategies you can use to increase the coherence of your writing even more.

1. *Plan the piece before you write it.* The easiest way to plan is to develop an outline. This does not necessarily mean using Roman numerals, capital letters, and so on. (Of course, if you feel comfortable using them, then by all means do so.) It means arranging the ideas that will appear in your paper, deciding which will come first, which second, and so on. The easiest way to do this is to study the ideas you have on your rough-idea sheet and *number them in the most effective order.* The following guidelines will help you decide what that order is:

The introduction to your paper should identify the essential features of the issue and present a careful statement of your judgment.* If possible, this should be done in an imaginative way that arouses reader interest and creates a positive impression as it informs.

*Skilled writers often withhold the complete statement of the judgment until later in the paper, sometimes at the very end, but this approach is not recommended for beginning writers.

The body of your paper should develop and support your judgment, presenting the various considerations that underlie that judgment and discussing the various questions and objections that might occur to critical readers. Useful patterns of organization for the middle of the paper include *time order* (you might, for example, discuss the effects of an action in the order in which they would occur in time), *order of complexity* (simpler considerations first, followed by more complex ones), and *order of importance* (less important considerations first, followed by more important ones).

The conclusion of your paper should reinforce the main idea (your judgment). This reinforcement is usually not accomplished by direct repetition (except in rather long treatments—say, more than 3,000 words). Instead, you should use a more subtle method, such as the use of an apt quotation or a statement of your own that recalls the main idea without using the same words.

2. *Decide what connecting words or phrases will make clear the relationships between your ideas, and add them to the numbers on your rough-idea sheet.* The basic relationships among ideas in persuasive writing are *and* relationships, *but* relationships, and *therefore* relationships. These relationships exist whether or not they are expressed. By expressing them, you make it possible for your readers to move from one idea to another without confusion and help them understand your reasoning more easily. To indicate the basic relationships you may use the words *and, but,* and *therefore* themselves or substitute words. Some common substitutes for *and* are *also, first, second, in addition, next, another,* and *finally.* For *but,* you may use *however, nevertheless, yet, in contrast,* and *on the other hand.* For *therefore,* you may use *so, consequently, accordingly, thus, as a result,* and *in conclusion.* Other relationship words that are helpful in making your writing more coherent are *for example* (to illustrate a point), *now* and *then* (to signal a time change), and *similarly* (to compare). At times a single word or phrase will not do, and you will have to add a complete sentence to make the connection clear.

How to Achieve Emphasis

(EMPH)

Emphasis is stress or prominence. A word, sentence, or paragraph has emphasis if it stands out from other words, sentences, or paragraphs in a piece of writing. Not every part is deserving of the same emphasis, so the careful writer controls the placement of emphasis. The following guidelines will help you exercise such control in your writing:

Assign an important idea *more space* than other ideas. If you discuss three considerations in a moral issue and give each consideration the same amount of space (say, a couple of sentences or a paragraph apiece), the subtle implication to your readers will be that all considerations are of equal importance. On the other hand, if you give one consideration more detailed treatment, that consideration will seem more important than the others. The space given to the development of each consideration should not be left to chance; it should be consciously chosen.

Assign an important idea *better space* than other ideas. Not every place in a piece of writing carries the same emphasis. Generally speaking, *the end has the greatest emphasis* because whatever is read last will usually be remembered longest. "End" in this context does not mean conclusion only. It means the final position of any sentence, any paragraph, or any section of a piece of writing (the body, for example). The construction of individual sentences that observe the principle of emphasis may be a little difficult for the beginning writer, but you should be able to make the final sentences of your paragraphs, the final paragraph of your body, and your conclusion more emphatic. *The place of second greatest emphasis is the beginning* because first impressions tend to last. Accordingly, the beginnings of sentences, of paragraphs, or of any section of a piece of writing (the body, for example) are important places. If you have a number of considerations to discuss in the body of your paper, it will usually be possible to use both the beginning and the end positions to achieve maximum emphasis. For example, begin with the second most important consideration, then turn to the lesser considerations, and end with the most important one.

Use repetition, echo words, and underlining judiciously. (Echo words are words that do not repeat what was said, but are so close in meaning that they recall it; *courage,* for example, might be used as an echo word for *bravery.*) The key word here is *judiciously.* To use any of these devices carelessly, particularly repetition, will distract and even offend the critical reader.

How to Develop Your Ideas
(DEV)

Developing your ideas means adding more words, lengthening your treatment of the case or issue. However, unlike padding, developing is not adding words just for the sake of adding them. It is *purposeful* enlargement of your treatment, which enhances its persuasiveness by removing any confusion or misunderstanding your readers might experience, by fulfilling their desire to know more about your judgment and the reasoning that underlies it, and by answering any doubts or objections they might have. There are two steps to follow in the development of your ideas:

1. *Look at your rough-idea sheet and determine which of your ideas might be misunderstood or disputed by your readers.* To perform this step effectively, you must get beyond your own perspective. (From that perspective every one of your ideas will seem unquestionable simply because it is your idea.) You must adopt a critical perspective and see your ideas as your readers, who are unfamiliar with them and uncommitted to them, will see them.

2. *Decide which techniques of development will best overcome confusion or answer objections.* The following techniques are especially helpful in a variety of situations:

Detailed description. This consists of a more specific presentation of the considerations in the case. For example, instead of merely stating that a certain consequence is likely to result, you would show why it is likely and exactly how it would happen, step by step.

Brief or extended illustration. This consists of offering examples, cases in point, to support your assertions. Instead of saying that the effects of a certain action would be harmful to the people involved, you would give examples of the harm that would (or might) be done. Illustrations may be actual examples that occurred in similar situations or hypothetical examples (plausible speculations).

Definition. This technique is helpful whenever you are using a term in a special sense or a way that might be misunderstood.

Comparison. This consists of evaluating the relative strengths and weaknesses of two or more different lines of reasoning about a case.

Explanation. This technique is useful for answering the questions that you anticipate your readers will ask. Common questions are why you consider a particular illustration typical, why you choose one interpretation over other possible ones, and why you believe that one consideration in a case (an obligation, for example) outweighs all others.

Tracing and summarizing. These techniques are more commonly used in advanced ethical treatments, but you may find them appropriate to some of your treatments. *Tracing* consists of briefly presenting the historical development of an idea or perspective. *Summarizing* consists of presenting a capsule version of some material that is too long to use in its original form. One of the most common uses of it in ethical analysis is to present the reasoning of ethicists to reinforce your analysis of a particular case.

How to Write Readable Prose
(STYLE)

Readable prose is prose that people find interesting, even pleasurable, to read. To some extent interest lies in the taste of the individual reader. What one person finds interesting will put another to sleep. Nevertheless, there are at least three qualities that tend to generate or at least increase enthusiasm among readers, qualities associated with energy and vitality rather than with dullness and monotony. Those qualities are exactness, economy, and liveliness. Here are some guidelines to help you achieve them in your writing.

To Achieve Exactness

1. Avoid empty or overworked expressions. It is easy to acquire the habit of expressing your thoughts in clichés or in currently fashionable phrasing. To break that habit, take note of your language. If you find it filled with the kind of phrasing you hear many times each day, make an effort to substitute more meaningful phrasing.

2. Prefer concrete, specific terms to abstract, general ones. It is not always possible in ethical analysis to avoid abstraction or generality, but it is important to do so whenever you can. Keep in mind that the purpose of writing in ethics, like the purpose of any writing, is to make your thoughts clear to others, not to befuddle them.

181

To Achieve Economy

1. Choose words to communicate your thoughts, not to impress your readers. Somehow many people have gotten the notion that fancy language and jargon will make them seem knowledgeable. The truth is quite the opposite; such language only makes them seem foolish. The right approach was best summed up by the distinguished essayist and novelist George Orwell when he said, *"Never use a long word where a short word will do."*

2. Wherever possible without sacrificing meaning, reduce a sentence to a clause, a clause to a phrase, a phrase to a word. (This does not prevent you from developing your ideas. Development is adding content, not multiplying words unnecessarily.)

To Achieve Liveliness

1. Control the rhythm and pace of your phrasing. Rhythm refers to the melodiousness of your writing, pace to the relative speed at which it moves. By reading your writing *aloud*, you can get a good idea of whether your writing is lively to read, whether it not only looks good, but sounds good as well. If your writing does not sound good when read aloud, try changing the phrasing of rough passages (to improve the rhythm) and moderating the sentence and paragraph length (to improve the pace).

2. Use vivid language in place of bland, predictable language. This guideline must be used with care, of course. Vividness can add a dramatic quality to your writing that will increase its liveliness, but if you use it carelessly, it will undermine exactness. To use it effectively, be sure the vivid expression does not represent an idea you cannot defend.

3. Vary your sentence style and your paragraph length. The essential ingredient in boredom is *sameness*. By reducing the degree of sameness in your writing, you overcome monotony and increase liveliness. Examine your sentences and paragraphs whenever you write. If the sentence length is unvaried, change it; make some sentences longer, some shorter. If all your sentences begin in much the same way, change the order of phrases or clauses or move an adverb around. Similarly, if your paragraphs are all the same length, and especially if they are all long, your paper will appear monotonous even before it is read. With a little skillful adjusting, you can usually achieve some variety in paragraph length without awkwardly separating related ideas. (A good average length for your paragraphs is ten lines, with variations from perhaps five to fifteen lines.)

One final note. Throughout this section we have been discussing rhetorical principles, but we have not mentioned grammar and usage. The reason for this is not that those concerns are unimportant, but that they cannot be treated adequately in a brief appendix. Critical readers may overlook an occasional lapse in grammar and usage. However, numerous errors will create a formidable distraction and suggest to readers that you are a careless person. Such a suggestion will hardly help your efforts to persuade readers of the soundness of your views. To make the best impression on your readers, see that any grammatical errors are corrected before you complete your final draft. A good dictionary is an indispensable tool for this task.

NOTES

CHAPTER 1

1. "New Law Sides with Rape Victim," *Oneonta* (New York) *Star*, July 23, 1982, p. 11.

2. Greg Brown, "Mutilated Voodoo Dolls Found in Delaware," *Oneonta Star*, July 23, 1982, p.1.

3. "Couple Who Let Baby Die Guilty," *Binghamton* (New York) *Press*, May 18, 1982, p. 5A.

4. "Zoo Kills Two Bears for Lack of a Home," *Oneonta Star*, May 15, 1982, p. 1.

5. "Right to Liberty," *New York Times*, April 25, 1982, p. 49.

6. *Binghamton Press*, August 7, 1982, p. 4A.

7. *Time*, June 26, 1972, pp. 74–75.

CHAPTER 2

1. Clyde Kluckhohn, *Mirror for Man* (New York: McGraw-Hill, 1949), pp. 18–19.

2. May and Abraham Edel, *Anthropology and Ethics* (Springfield, Ill.: Charles C. Thomas, 1959), pp. 88–89.

3. Ruth Benedict, *Patterns of Culture* (Cambridge, Mass.: Riverside Press; and Boston: Houghton Mifflin, 1934), pp. 45–46.

4. Benedict, *Patterns of Culture,* pp. 210, 216.

5. Ibid., Chapter 5.

6. Kluckhohn, *Mirror for Man,* p. 41.

7. Ibid., pp. 177–78.

8. Benedict, *Patterns of Culture,* p. 172.

9. Edel, *Anthropology and Ethics,* pp. 88–89.

CHAPTER 3

1. All three cases are referred to by Louis Lasagna in "Special Subjects in Human Experimentation," *Daedalus,* Winter 1969, p. 449.

CHAPTER 4

1. *New York Times,* June 14, 1981, p. 28.

2. *Facts on File: 1971,* Vol. XXXI, No. 1588, p. 248.

3. *Facts on File: 1956,* Vol. XVI, No. 800, p. 68.

CHAPTER 5

1. "White Slavery, 1972," *Time,* June 5, 1972, p. 24.

2. "Mummy Removed from Public View," *New York Times,* September 10, 1972, p. 42.

3. "He's Cashing In on the Jobless Trend," *Los Angeles Times,* April 21, 1982, Part V, p. 1.

4. "Nassau Officer Pleads Guilty . . . ," *New York Times,* April 18, 1982, p. 45.

5. "Two Accused of Selling Unborn Babe," *Oneonta Star,* July 23, 1982, p. 20.

CHAPTER 6

1. T. W. Adorno et al., *The Authoritarian Personality* (New York: Harper & Brothers, 1950), pp. 147–48.

2. Else Frenkel-Brunswik, "Prejudice in Children," *Psychology in Action,* ed. Fred McKinney (New York: Macmillan, 1967), pp. 276–90.

3. "Priest Picketed for Drowning Cats," *Oneonta Star,* February 19, 1982, p. 2.

CHAPTER 7

1. "Respect for Persons," *Daedalus*, Spring 1969, p. 113.
2. "Introduction to the Issue 'Ethical Aspects of Experimentation with Human Subjects,' " *Daedalus*, Spring 1969, p. x.
3. Ibid.
4. Geoffrey Edsall, "A Positive Approach to the Problem of Human Experimentation," *Daedalus*, Spring 1969, pp. 470–71.
5. Jack Anderson, "Army Scientists Move Closer to Orwell's 1984," *Oneonta Star*, August 5, 1972, p. 5.

CHAPTER 8

1. *The Right and the Good* (Oxford: Clarendon Press, 1930), Chap. 2.
2. "The AEC and Secrecy," *Time*, August 14, 1972, p. 73.

CHAPTER 9

1. "Hollow Holiness," *Time*, August 14, 1972, p. 45.
2. "Cop Suspended for Nude Photos," *Oneonta Star*, July 31, 1982, p. 9.
3. "Hundreds Reply to Pregnancy Cost Ad," *New York Times*, August 13, 1972, p. 67.
4. "Road to Survival a Gruesome Path," *Oneonta Star*, December 27, 1972, p. 1.

CHAPTER 10

1. Henry K. Beecher, "Scarce Resources and Medical Advancement," *Daedalus*, Spring 1969, pp. 280–81.

CHAPTER 11

1. "Seven-Year-Old Boy Charged . . . ," *Oneonta Star*, July 22, 1982, p. 2.
2. "Husband Says Wife Begged for Death," *Oneonta Star*, July 31, 1982, p. 2.
3. "Five Teens Charged in Fatal Derailment," *Oneonta Star*, July 9, 1982, p. 1.

CONTEMPORARY ETHICAL CONTROVERSIES

Education

1. *New York Times*, August 22, 1982, Section 4, p. 20.

2. " 'Lesbianism' Charges Prompt Course Review," *Oneonta Star*, July 19, 1982, p. 2.

3. *New York Times*, November 26, 1972, p. 41.

Media and the Arts

1. Karen Stabiner, "Tapping the Homosexual Market," *New York Times Magazine*, May 5, 1982, pp. 34ff.

Sex

1. "Under the Yum-Yum Tree?" *Binghamton Press*, December 12, 1972, p. 1.

2. Boyce Rensberger, "Clinics for Sex Therapy Proliferate over Nation," *New York Times*, October 29, 1972, p. 1.

3. Ibid., p. 66.

4. Ibid.

5. "1986: A Space Odyssey to Mars," *Time*, December 11, 1972, p. 47.

Government

1. "SBA Sex Palace Loan Irks Reformers," *Oneonta Star*, June 10, 1982, p. 2.

2. "U.S. Recruited Nazis in Spy Network," *Oneonta Star*, May 17, 1982, p. 1.

3. George Bria, " 'Tens of Thousands' Are Still Enslaved," *Binghamton Press*, October 28, 1972, p. 4.

4. Walter Sullivan, "The Lady Was 2,000 Years Old," *New York Times*, August 6, 1972, Section 4, p. 9.

Law

1. "Taser Gun 'Wilts' Feisty Prisoners," *Oneonta Star*, June 26, 1982, p. 1.

2. "The Lawyer of Last Resort," *Time*, May 17, 1982, p. 64.

Business

1. "Products Unsafe at Home Are Still Unloaded Abroad," *New York Times*, August 22, 1982, Section 4, p. 9.

2. "U.S. Charges Nineteen . . . ," *Oneonta Star*, June 23, 1982, p. 1.

3. Jack Anderson, "Double Suicide," *Oneonta Star*, November 24, 1972, p. 4.

Medicine

1. "Burn Victim Shuffled for Lack of Insurance," *Oneonta Star*, May 10, 1982, p. 12.

2. " 'Doctor, Do We Have a Choice?' " *New York Times Magazine*, January 30, 1972, p. 24.

3. "Philosophical Reflections on Human Experimentation," *Daedalus*, Spring 1969, p. 244.

4. "Society Speed," *Time*, December 18, 1972, pp. 76–77.

Notes

Science

1. Rick Scott, "Indians Charge Heritage Plundered, Flooded Out," *Oneonta Star*, October 2, 1972, p. 1.

2. Jane Brody, "All in the Name of Science," *New York Times*, July 30, 1972, Section 4, p. 6.

3. "Philosophical Reflections on Human Experimentation," *Daedalus*, Spring 1969, pp. 229ff.

4. "The Ethical Design of Human Experiments," *Daedalus*, Spring 1969, p. 529.

5. Ibid., p. 524.

War

1. "Now, the Death Ray?" *Time*, September 4, 1972, p. 46.